UNIQUE New England

A Guide to the Region's Quirks, Charisma, and Character

Sarah Lovett

John Muir Publications
Santa Fe, New Mexico

Special thanks to Peggy van Hulsteyn, Ellen Thompson, Steve Justis, Vermont Department of Agriculture, Aaron Schmidt, Boston Public Library, Phoebe Phillips, Connecticut Historical Society, Rhode Island Tourism Division, New Hampshire Office of Travel & Tourism Development, Massachusetts Office of Tourism, Vermont Travel Division, Connecticut Dept. of Economic Development, and Maine Office of Tourism.

John Muir Publications, P.O. Box 613, Santa Fe, NM 87504
© 1994 by Sarah Lovett
Cover © 1994 by John Muir Publications
All rights reserved. Published 1994.
Printed in the United States of America

First edition. First printing March 1994.

Library of Congress Cataloging-in-Publication Data
Lovett, Sarah, 1953–
Unique New England : a guide to the region's quirks, charisma, and character / by Sarah lovett.
   p.   cm.
   Includes index.
ISBN 1-56261-146-1 : $10.95
1. New England—Guidebooks. I. Title.
F2.3.L68 1994
917.404'43—dc20   93-32352
                                 CIP

Design: Ken Wilson
Typography: Marcie Pottern
Illustrations: Bette Brodsky
Photo and Text Research: Timothy Thompson
Typeface: Belwe, Oz Handicraft
Printer: Malloy Lithographing

Distributed to the book trade by
W. W. Norton & Co.
New York, New York

Cover photo © Leo de Wys, Inc./Everett C. Johnson
Cover photo inset © Leo de Wys, Inc./Henry K. Kaiser
Back cover photo © Joseph St. Pierre

CONTENTS

INTRODUCTION

Think of covered bridges, cranberries, Yankees, and moose. That's New England, right? Of course, there are many other things to discover about the region. For instance, did you know that New England is an important stopover for migrating birds traveling the Atlantic Flyway? And that you can beachcomb or sunbathe on thousands of miles of ocean shoreline? And that New England's wineries produce award-winning wines (including cranberry and peach) as well as English-style ciders?

Unique New England is a compilation of fascinating destinations, key facts, quick-reference maps, and fun trivia. Where else can you find a recipe for fish chowder, a map of historic and contemporary taverns, and a chart of the best lobster-eating techniques?

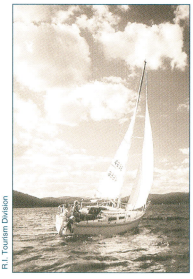

R.I. Tourism Division

Sailing off Rhode Island shores

Open to any page and you will find readable, entertaining information. The index guides you to specific topics and sites. The contents is organized so that you can tell at a glance what subjects are covered in each section. However you choose to use this book, you'll soon discover what is unique about New England.

Boston Public Library

Firefighters in Boston, ca. 1890

Project Puffin

In 1973, the sum total of puffin eggs in the state of Maine could be found at Matinicus Rock and Machias Seal Island. The National Audubon Society began the **Puffin Project** in an attempt to restore puffins to former nesting islands in the Gulf of Maine. Happily, puffins are not endangered birds, but they are rare to Maine. The Society's restoration efforts at Eastern Egg Rock in Muscongus Bay and Seal Island have both been successful. June and July are the best puffin-watching months. Island visits are limited and must be made by reservation. *FYI:* National Audubon Society, HC 60, Box 102-P, Medomak, ME 04551; Maine Audubon Society, 207-781-2330.

Joseph Devenney/Maine Office of Tourism

A puffin munches on a fish

New England States Trivia Quiz

1) _____ is the nation's most densely populated and smallest state.
   a) Vermont **b** Rhode Island **c)** Connecticut
2) A total of 18 coastal miles are found in _____.
   a) New Hampshire **b)** Vermont **c)** Maine
3) The _____ (many still live in Massachusetts) is one of New England's principal Native American tribes.
   a) Wampanoag **b)** Apache **c)** Seminole
4) _____ is known as the "Constitution State."
   a) New Hampshire **b)** Massachusetts **c)** Connecticut
5) _____ produces the nation's largest cranberry crop.
   a) Rhode Island **b)** Vermont **c)** Massachusetts
6) _____ is sometimes called "Downeast" because of prevailing winds that send ocean vessels eastward.
   a) Connecticut **b)** Maine **c)** Vermont
7) The _____ is Massachusetts' official state flower.
   a) wallflower **b)** wheat flower **c)** mayflower

ANSWERS: 1) b 2) a 3) a 4) c 5) c 6) b 7) c

THEN AND NOW

30,000 B.C.–1600s

First People

While some believe that Paleo-Indians were present in North America as long ago as 35,000 years, the generally accepted number is 11,000 years. Whether these ancient hunters originally traveled from the north or the south is debated. Scholars who support the north-to-south theory believe Asians crossed the Bering Strait 15,000 years ago. Those who subscribe to the theory that early South and Central American residents migrated north base their belief on archaeological evidence demonstrating cultural commonalities between early North Americans and South and Central Americans. Whatever their path, native peoples were well established in present-day New England when Norse Vikings reached North America around 1000 B.C.

The Vikings probably attempted to establish settlements in the land they called "Vinland," but they found that the indigenous people fiercely defended their homeland. Apparently, the Nordics withdrew to more secure settlements in Iceland and Greenland.

Nearly 500 years after the Vikings arrived in New England, European nations were competing for new lands to exploit. In 1492, Columbus set forth on his historic voyage to the New World, and other explorers soon followed. In 1497, John Cabot (born Giovanni Caboto) claimed all of present-day New England for the English king, Henry VII. More than a century later, England's George Weymouth, Thomas Hunt, and others explored the region, but Capt. John Smith was the first to seriously consider colonizing the land he named New England.

Pilgrims and Plymouth Rock

On September 15, 1620, the *Mayflower* sailed from England; on board were Puritans in search of religious freedom. In November, the ship reached what is now Provincetown. There, the Puritans drafted and signed the Mayflower Compact, their governing charter based on

Mass. Office of Tourism & Old Sturbridge Village

Harvest at the Plimouth Plantation, Plymouth, Mass.

majority volition. They continued on to Plymouth Rock, south of Massachusetts Bay, where they landed just four days before Christmas. Disease and harsh winter conditions left half of the party dead, but those who survived found luck in the form of a Pawtuxet man named Squanto. Because he had learned English when he was taken to England by explorers, Squanto was able to act as translator and diplomat for the Puritans.

As colonists continued to arrive from England, settlements spread north and south into more fertile lands. In 1630, Puritan John Winthrop established the Massachusetts Bay settlement that would be known as Boston.

Squanto (?-1622)

Squanto (also known as Tisquantum), a member of the Pawtuxet tribe, was kidnapped by English Capt. Thomas Hunt in 1615, taken to

England, and returned to his homeland in 1619 by Capt. Thomas Dermer. Squanto is also believed by some to have been abducted from Maine by George Weymouth, taken to England, and returned by John Smith in 1615.

In 1621, Squanto aided the negotiation of a fifty-year peace treaty between the Puritans and Wampanoag *sachem* (chief) Massasoit. He continued to assist the growing Puritan settlements, especially with fishing and planting. Squanto died of smallpox in 1622 while acting as a guide on William Bradford's expedition around Cape Cod.

1600–1700

Roger Williams (ca. 1603–1683)

Roger Williams was born in London, the son of a merchant tailor. After studying law and theology at Cambridge University, Williams gained a controversial reputation as a minister who opposed the established English church. Williams was welcomed in Boston in 1631, but four years later he was banished from the Massachusetts Bay Colony because he challenged the religious dogma of the Puritans and condemned the taking of Indian lands.

Williams and a few followers founded Providence—in what would soon be known as the colony of Rhode Island—after the land was given to him by his friends, Narragansett chiefs Canonicus and Miantunomi. The settlement became a "lively experiment" in religious freedom and an affirmation of William's contest for liberty. The 4½-acre Roger Williams National Memorial in downtown Providence commemorates the man who was a statesman, free thinker, and ardent defender of American Indian legal rights. *FYI:* 282 N. Main Street, Providence, RI 02903.

C. Browning/R.I. Tourism Division

Benefit Street, Providence, R.I.

King Philip's War, 1675–1676

Wampanoag Chief Wamsutta, son of Chief Massasoit, may have been murdered by the English. Wamsutta's brother Metacom, also known as King Philip, became the new sachem, and he managed to keep the peace with colonists for several years. As Indian dependence on colonial goods increased—as did the forced sale of Indian lands to colonists—so did hostilities between whites and native tribes. Wamsutta complied with an English demand that Indians give up their arms.

In 1675, a Christian Native American and probable British informer was murdered; three Wampanoag men were tried for the crime and executed. This spurred an Indian attack the same year when Wampanoags raided the settlement of Swansea. Native Americans and whites engaged in escalating acts of violence until additional tribes and all the New England colonies were drawn into war. Two events led to the defeat of Metacom's cause: his attempt to enlist the support of the Mohawk failed, and his allies, the Narragansetts, were defeated and their leader, Canonchet, was killed by the colonists.

Metacom went into hiding at Mt. Hope (Bristol, Rhode Island). In August 1676, he was killed by a Native American who was working for English Capt. Benjamin Church. Metacom's wife and son were captured, and the dead chief's body was drawn and quartered; his head was impaled on a post and publicly displayed in Plymouth.

Although the cost of war was high for the colonists in terms of dollars and human life, it cleared the way for white expansion into tribal homeland. For the Indians, the consequence of this war was the extermination of tribal life in southern New England.

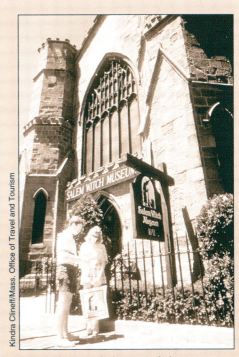

Kindra Clineff/Mass. Office of Travel and Tourism

The infamous Salem witch hunts began in 1692, and historians still do not agree on the cause of this strange and fanatical period of American history. Today, the curious and the scholarly stop at the Salem Witch Museum, Salem, Mass.

1700–1783

The Stamp Act, the Boston Tea Party, and Revolution!

When King George III imposed the Revenue Act of 1764 on New England and followed it a year later with the Stamp Act, citizens were vocal in their opposition to new taxes. Although the Stamp Act was repealed in March 1766, England had not learned its lesson. In 1767, the Townsend Acts imposed severe duties on tea, paper, and other colonial imports. In response to the New Englanders' resistance, British troops landed at Boston. When they clashed with a crowd of Bostonians on March 5, 1770, shots were fired by Redcoats, and five colonists, including Crispus Attucks, were mortally wounded. These were the revolution's first martyrs, killed in what became known as the Boston Massacre.

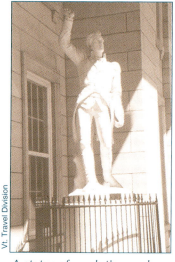

Vt. Travel Division

A statue of revolutionary hero Ethan Allen, leader of the Green Mountain Boys, stands in Montpelier, Vt.

Although British Parliament repealed the Townsend Acts, a tax on East India tea was left in effect. Men such as Samuel Adams and James Otis spoke out passionately against taxation in Boston's **Faneuil Hall** and **Old South Meeting House.**

On December 16, 1773, a band of sixty men disguised as Mohawk Indians boarded English ships in Boston Harbor and dumped more than 300 crates of tea into the water.

By May 1774, British troops had occupied Boston, and on April 18, 1775, Paul Revere and William Dawes galloped to Lexington to warn Samuel Adams, John Hancock, and the Minutemen of the advancing British attack. The shots heard on Lexington Green and Concord's North Bridge on April 19 signaled the beginning of the **Battle of Lexington,** the **Battle of Concord**, and the war for independence.

The revolution's first major battle, the **Battle of Bunker Hill,** was fought on June 17, 1775, on the Charleston peninsula. In an effort to control overland access to Boston, British regulars held control of the peninsula hills. On June 16, American Col. William Prescott led 1,200 colonial militiamen to fortify Bunker's Hill; in fact, Prescott's troops hunkered down at Breed's Hill, which was closer to Boston. The next morning, British Gen. Gage gave the command to capture the position. British regulars faced fierce fighting from the ragtag colonial militia; they managed to scale Breed's Hill on the third try.

The British victory was costly: 1,304 casualties out of 2,200 soldiers. The 2,500 to 4,000 colonials lost between 400 and 600 soldiers; they also learned they would need strong leadership to win future battles. On July 3, 1775, George Washington took over as commander in chief of the new Continental Army.

Mass. Office of Travel and Tourism

This etching depicts the Old West Church (on Lynde and Cambridge streets, Boston) ca. 1853.

Historic Footsteps

For a historic tour of eighteenth- and nineteenth-century Boston, allow the better part of a day to walk the 2½-mile **Freedom Trail** connecting the 16 sites that compose the **Boston National Historic Park.** As you follow the red line in the sidewalk past the Old South Meeting House (the birthplace of the Boston Tea Party), Old State House (the site of the Boston Massacre), and Bunker Hill Monument, you will simultaneously be visiting modern Boston's varied neighborhoods, the Italian North End, the Irish Charlestown, and the fashionable Beacon Hill. The **Black Heritage Trail** winds through sites of Beacon Hill's nineteenth-century black community. *FYI:* National Park Service, 15 State Street, Boston, Mass.; 617-223-5200.

War, Independence, and New Trade

Colonial troops had rallied at Bennington, Vermont, even before the revolution officially began in April 1775. Bennington was also the gathering place of the Green Mountain Boys and Ethan Allen, who joined Benedict Arnold and his troops on their march to Fort Ticonderoga, which they captured from the British in 1775.

In August 1777, the important **Battle of Bennington** was fought nearby. Desperate for supplies, British Gen. John Burgoyne had sent troops to Bennington to seize munitions. Already apprised of the attack, Gen. John Stark from New Hampshire led the colonial militia to head off the enemy. The forces clashed at the site of Wallomsac Heights, New York, and the British suffered a disastrous defeat. Although many revolutionary war battles were fought in New York and Pennsylvania, New England was the start of it all. *FYI:* Patriots Day, April 19, is a Massachusetts holiday. Locals and visitors alike gather to watch reenactments of the battles of Lexington and Concord staged by uniformed volunteers.

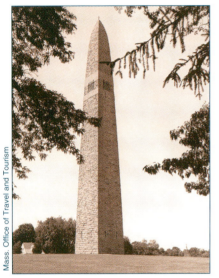

The Battle of Bennington Monument

Mass. Office of Travel and Tourism

George Washington (1732–1799)

George Washington was born on February 22, 1732, on the family estate in Virginia. Wealth and ambition furthered Washington's career aspirations, and he was appointed to his first public office in 1749 at the age of seventeen. By the age of twenty, Major Washington was placed in charge of training the militia under his command. He won his first military victory against French forces in 1754 during the French and Indian Wars. In 1759, Washington married Martha Dandridge Custic and settled at Mt. Vernon.

At the start of the American Revolution, Washington was named commander in chief of the Continental Army. He took command of an unorganized, poorly disciplined force of men on July 3, 1775, at Cambridge, Massachusetts. His challenge was to hold fast the British while training his men in the field; at the same time, he faced congressional interference. Although he was victorious in forcing the British to evacuate Boston on March 17, 1776, the war was far from over.

Nathan Hale (1755–1776)

Nathan Hale, born in Coventry, Connecticut, was a schoolteacher when the American Revolution began. Commissioned as an officer in the Connecticut militia, Hale fought in the siege of Boston. He volunteered to gather information on Britain's forces on Long Island. It was a dangerous mission, and when Hale was captured, he was hanged without a trial. He is known as a hero of the American

Revolution.

Trade

With American independence came new trade opportunities for New England's merchants. Whaling and trading vessels were built in Maine, Rhode Island, Massachusetts, and Connecticut. They returned from long voyages laden with whale oil and goods from China, Africa, Europe, and India. They also brought new prosperity for the region.

Arms

In 1777, the Springfield Armory in Springfield, Massachusetts, was selected by Gen. George Washington as the location of the first U.S. arsenal; the armory developed military small arms for 190 years. Most famous for crafting the percussion rifle musket, the main arsenal houses the world's largest collection of small arms. *FYI:* One Armory Square, Springfield, MA 01105.

1783–1880

Industrial Revolution

Samuel Slater arrived in New England in 1789 and established a cotton-spinning mill in Pawtucket, Rhode Island. The same type of machinery design that was making the British rich also worked for Slater in the New World.

New mills and industrial factories sprouted along New England's rivers like weeds. Homes, stores, civic buildings, and churches soon followed the factories until entire towns were built from the textile, machinery, tool and instrument, and leather industries— and from Yankee ingenuity.

Browning/R.I. Tourism Division

In the late 1700s, Samuel Slater established a cotton mill in Rhode Island. This marked the beginning of New England's textile industry.

Boston Public Library

Considered to be the birthplace of the American Industrial Revolution, the central Massachusetts mill towns of Worcester, Millbury, Sutton, Grafton, Northbridge, Uxbridge, Millville, and Blackstone shipped manufactured goods and farm produce by way of the Blackstone Canal, which is in the process of being restored. Today, along with hiking and canoeing, the park offers demonstrations of nineteenth-century industrial processes such as the making of wool at the Stanley Woolen Mill in Uxbridge.

FYI: **Blackstone River and Canal Heritage State Park,** 21 Mendon Street, P.O. Box 405, Uxbridge, MA 01569.

This balloon view of Boston on October 13, 1860, was the first aerial photograph taken in the United States

Celebrating the Industrial Revolution of the 1850s, summer boat and trolley tours at **Lowell National Historic Park** take visitors back in time to restored canals, mills, worker housing and nineteenth-century commercial buildings. The park's visitor center features changing exhibits memorializing the workers of the Industrial Revolution; the center is open year-round. *FYI:* Visitor's Center, 246 Market Street, Lowell, MA 01852.

Harriet Beecher Stowe (1811–1896)

Harriet Beecher Stowe was born in Litchfield, Connecticut; in 1826, her family moved to Boston and then settled in Cincinnati in 1832. Stowe influenced the course of American history when she wrote the most controversial and widely read novel of the nineteenth century, *Uncle Tom's Cabin*. The book was Stowe's response to the Fugitive Slave Law of 1850. It was an instant bestseller and brought the author fame and notoriety. After its publication, Stowe traveled to England where she met prominent women writers such as Elizabeth Gaskell and Elizabeth Barrett Browning.

Boston Public Library

Stowe's mother died when she was four. Her father, Calvinist minister Lyman Beecher, wrote to a friend, "Hattie is a genius. I would give a hundred dollars if she was a boy." Her most famous sibling was pulpit orator Henry Ward Beecher. In her early teens, Stowe had a conversion experience; by 18, she was a committed Calvinist. More than thirty years later, she converted to Episcopalianism, her mother's religion.

In addition to her novels, Stowe wrote short stories and domestic manuals. Among her novels are *The Minister's Wooing* (1859), *The Pearl of Orr's Island* (1862), and *Oldtown Folks* (1868). She also wrote *Dred: A Tale of the Great Dismal Swamp* (1856), which explores the effects of slavery on white perpetrators, and *Lady Byron Vindicated* (1870), a controversial defense of the reputation of Lord Byron's maligned widow.

Twentieth Century

The twentieth century heralded the end of the commercial boom and brought financial hardship and a diminishing job market to New England. Factories moved their operations South where production costs were lower, New England farmers found themselves out-produced by vast agricultural endeavors in more fertile regions of the nation, and millions of immigrants who had come to the Northeast during the boom of the 1800s were without training. But new opportunities arose after World War II. New England's plentiful colleges and universities moved to the educational forefront, commercial fishing boats pulled plentiful seafood from Atlantic waters, and the area's rich history attracted visitors.

New England today is renowned for its beautiful landscapes, autumn colors, history, technical and medical research, and livability.

Boston Public Library

The 1911 graduating class at the Plymouth Hospital Training School for Nurses

New Boston

The twentieth century brought deterioration to Boston; higher taxes, a lower population, and the exit of businesses meant urban blight was taking its toll. The **Boston Redevelopment Authority** was established in 1957 to initiate revitalization of the city. MIT architect I. M. Pei was hired to design a renewed city. A new City Hall built in close proximity to government, commercial, and residential buildings formed the heart of the project. For several decades, I. M. Pei and associates continued to be part of the project. Today, neighborhoods of Boston are still being transformed by conscious expansion.

John Fitzgerald Kennedy (1917–1963)

John Fitzgerald Kennedy was born in Brookline, Massachusetts, one of nine children of the prosperous Kennedy family. Kennedy was educated at Harvard and served as a PT-boat captain during World War II. He served as congressman and senator before his election as the thirty-fifth president of the United States in 1960. Kennedy was the youngest president and the first Roman Catholic ever to hold office.

John F. Kennedy Library

The **Beals Street house** in the Boston suburb where Kennedy was born has been restored to its 1917 appearance. Supervised by Rose Kennedy, John's mother, the home has been refurnished with many of the items actually used by the Kennedy family. After touring the house, you can take a neighborhood walk past St. Aidan's Church where JFK was baptized. You can also see Dexter School and the Edward Devotion School, both attended by Kennedy; these historic buildings date to the 1700s. *FYI:* **John Fitzgerald Kennedy National Historic Site**, 83 Beals Street, Brookline, MA 02146.

Boston Public Library

Calvin Coolidge (1872–1933)

Calvin Coolidge was born in Plymouth, Vermont. "Callow Cal," known for his honesty and popularity, served as Massachusetts state senator, lieutenant governor, and governor before he was elected vice president in the Harding administration. When Harding died in 1923, Coolidge became the thirtieth president of the United States.

THE NATURAL WORLD

Mt. Monadnock, N.H.

Boufford/N.H. Office of Travel & Tourism

Rock and Roll

New England covers a mere 66,672 square miles (172,680 sq. km) in the northeast corner of the United States. Much of the region's familiar terrain consists of valleys and rocky, rolling hills, while mountains and coastal shores form its borders. The White Mountains border the north, the Green Mountains and Taconic Range delineate the west, and the east is bounded by rocky shoreline.

Several billion years ago, the ancestors of the Green Mountains and the Taconics were created by uplift. Beneath the shallow inland sea that covered much of the earth's crust, tumult and upheaval caused a buckling along the Canadian shield and mountainous masses rose above the water. These ancient mountains may have been as high as the present-day Himalayas. Continued uplift and erosion reshaped the mountains, which were subsequently sculpted and scraped by glaciers. It was ice that created the New England landscape we see today.

Glaciers

At the dawn of the Cenozoic era—about 65 million years ago—the earth's climate cooled noticeably and glaciers began to form. Accumulations of snow became so weighty that the lowest layers were compressed into ice. When the ice reached a large enough mass, glaciers spread and reshaped whatever lay in their path. Steep valleys were modified and dammed, and the melted glaciers formed lakes. Ridges of debris—glacial moraines—left behind after the "meltdown" formed Cape Cod, Martha's Vineyard, Nantucket, Block Island, and Long Island. The final of four glacial stages ended roughly 10,000 years ago.

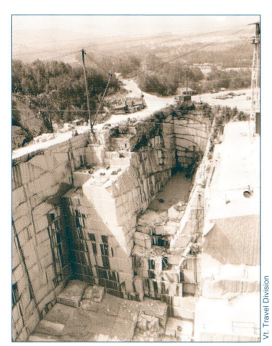

Vermont boasts the world's largest granite quarry

Vt. Travel Division

Land Features

The **Appalachian Mountains** reach more than 1,500 miles from the St. Lawrence Valley in Canada to Alabama and were formed about 8 million years ago. They include the **White Mountains,** the **Green Mountains,** the **Taconics,** the **Monadnocks.**

The 400-mile-long **Connecticut Valley** divides New England roughly in half north to south. The fossil-rich valley was created by faulting and subsequent repeated uplift.

The New England seacoast is splintered and jagged to the north, with numerous peninsulas. Bays and offshore islands resulted when glaciers melted and flooded the land. Sandy beaches are found south of Portland, Maine, and vast salt marshes provide safe habitat for birds traveling the **Atlantic Flyway.**

Making Tracks

Roughly 300 million years ago, dinosaurs roamed much of the North American continent, and they thrived in the area of New England now known as the Connecticut River Valley. At the end of the dinosaur age, a shallow sea covered much of New England. Dinosaur bones and tracks were preserved under layers of sediment deposited by the tides. Herbivores and carnivores alike left tracks in Triassic mud. *FYI:* Tracks are best seen at Dinosaur State Park, in Rocky Hill, Conn., and at South Hadley and Smith's Ferry,

All Ablaze

Fall foliage in East Topsham, Vt.

Vt. Travel Division

More than 75 percent of New England's surface is woodland. Summer greenery and fiery autumn foliage draw thousands of visitors to the area. Broad-leafed deciduous birch, hickory, oak, sugar maple, and beech trees share the forests with conifers such as spruce, white pine, and balsam fir.

Upwards of half a million people fill New England roadways during the first two weeks of October when **fall foliage** is ablaze. Red maples, scarlet oak, sassafras, and dogwoods flash their crimson leaves against the bright gold halo of poplars and birches and the orange glow of hickories. Maple trees are the superstar show-offs of this natural display. Although you may not be thinking about science when you view the hues, it is interesting to know that cold fall nights and sunny days trigger the cessation in a leaf's chlorophyll production, which in turn allows latent pigments such as tannin, carotene, and anthocynin to show their true colors. Although the leaves change from mid-September through late October, the first two weeks of October are the most sensational.

All Abloom

After the snow melts in the late spring, the countryside blossoms and bursts into assorted bloom—laurel and rhododendron are standouts. Summer flowers include goldenrod, buttercups, daisies, assorted asters, lupine, and turk's cap lily. Exotic lady slippers and jack-in-the-pulpits sprout up in moist marshland.

Odd Bogs

Swampy soil is no stranger to New England. Blame the wet stuff on ancient glaciers or on the ocean; either way, sedges, orchids, sphagnum moss, and other support plants are quick to occupy the acidic environment. Cranberries, too, take advantage of the bogs, and they have made possible a small industry that is unique to New England.

Because of the high acid pH of the marshlands, normal decay and breakdown are inhibited and eventually dead matter becomes peat. Over time, bog buildup may support shrubs and trees. Ultimately, forests will take over.

Seaweeds

Marine plants are abundant in New England's coastal waters. Seaweeds vary in size, color, and shape, but almost all reproduce via spores; broken pieces will grow into mature plants.

1) Cladophora: This small light green alga grows in tufts along rocks in tidal pools.

2) Oarweed: This large brown kelp—a source of iodine—is distinguished by its thick, flat blades. It is usually found in cold water below the low-tide line.

3) Rockweed: Also known as bladder wrack, this large brown alga grows profusely in the mid-tidal zone. Look for air bladders, usually in pairs, that keep this plant afloat.

4) Sea Lettuce: It really does look like lettuce; the thin green membranes grow from one to three feet across.

The Wild Life

Moose *(Alces alces)*

The mighty moose is the largest member of the deer family. Adult males may reach a head-to-tail length of more than 3 meters (10 feet), a shoulder height of almost 2.5 meters (8 feet), and a whopping weight of 825 kilograms (1,819 pounds). Antler spreads of 2 meters (6½ feet) have been recorded.

A Maine moose takes a refreshing break

Even if most of these animals don't sport six-foot antler spreads, it's not difficult to recognize moose in the wild. They are known for the characteristic square "hang-dog" muzzle as well as the slack flap of skin—known as the "bell"—beneath the throat.

Moose are active during the day, especially at dawn and dusk. They depend on acute senses of smell and hearing instead of their eyesight, which is poor. Generally, moose walk quietly through underbrush, but they can run as fast as 56 kilometers per hour (about 35 mph) when necessary.

They are able swimmers and often feed in lakes and streams, sometimes completely submerged so as to reach roots and stems of water plants.

Moose are solitary animals, although groups may gather in feeding areas during the late fall or winter. The fall is also the time for mating. Push and shove matches are common when two males compete for a female. Females are territorial, and they use sound and scent to attract males. The mating call of the female is a moan, while the male emits more of a croak. Lovesick moose have been known to dote on domestic cows, even on wooden deer.

While moose used to occupy much of Europe, Siberia, and North America, hunters had noticeably reduced their numbers in Europe by the thirteenth century. In North America, moose were almost exterminated by 1900. Today, a small but increasing population may be found in New England, especially in Maine.

American Black Bear *(Ursus americanus)*

The predominantly nocturnal American black bear is a fairly common resident of New England, although its range has been lessened considerably in other areas of North America.

Adept swimmers and climbers, black bears generally travel with an ungainly walk; they can move quickly when the need arises. They hibernate during the winter months— usually October to May— although they may emerge from burrows during warmer weather. Roughly two-thirds of the black bear's diet consists of vegetable matter,

including fruits, nuts, acorns, berries, grass, and roots. When available, they also eat fish, insects, rodents and larger mammals, and carrion.

June through July is the peak of the mating season. Births usually occur in January or February when the female is hibernating. Cubs are furless and blind at birth.

When startled, black bears emit a "woof." They are generally harmless to humans, except when they are wounded or protecting their young; there have been cases of human deaths inflicted by these mammals. Bears who have been fed by humans may become dangerous. Never try to feed bears or any other wild animals—it is harmful to you and to them.

Atlantic
Flyway

The Atlantic Flyway, the migration path of many species of birds, passes over New England

Life List

The Atlantic Flyway passes over New England's coastal marshes where numerous bird species find nourishment, rest, and nesting areas. Bird watchers are almost as thick as the birds near Barnstable Harbor, Cape Cod, where flat expanses of salt marsh attract spring and fall migrators such as Canada geese. Terns and seagulls are commonplace along the seacoast, and great cormorants share their cliff rock habitats with seals.

Birders can add numerous species of waterfowl and shorebirds to their life lists at any of the following refuges and sanctuaries:

The Nature Conservancy, Maine: The Great Wass Archipelago, southeast of Bangor, is known for its oceanic microclimate, which is colder and wetter than the mainland. Dovekies, common and king eiders, arctic terns, bald eagles, murres, goshawks, and red-tailed hawks are only a few of the birds seen on Great Wass Island. *FYI:* Fort Andross, 14 Maine Street, Suite 401, Brunswick, ME 04011; 207-729-5181.

Audubon Center and Audubon Fairchild Garden, Conn.: Miles of trails traverse this 280-acre refuge and educational center. Look for northern cardinals, rose-breasted grosbeaks, chickadees, and hawks. *FYI:* National Audubon Society, Audubon Center in Greenwich, 613 Riversville Road, Greenwich, CT 06831; 203-869-5272.

Ninigret National Wildlife Refuge Complex, R.I.: The 46-acre Block Island refuge is only a small portion of the Ninigret Refuge Complex, which also includes Trustom Pond, Ninigret, and Sachuest Point. Bird species number in the hundreds. *FYI:* Shoreline Plaza, Route 1A, P.O. Box 307, Charlestown, RI 02813; 401-364-9124.

Eastern Point Bird Sanctuary, Mass.: This sanctuary near Gloucester has roughly 25 acres of marshlands and coastal headlands that are species-rich when it comes to waterfowl and shorebirds.

Bartholomew's Cobble, Mass.: Hiking trails ramble through the natural rock garden and follow the bank of the Housatonic River. In the beautiful Berkshires, this is an excellent location for bird-watching. *FYI:* 413-229-8600; Sheffield.

Parker River Wildlife Refuge, Mass.: Six miles of dunes and sandy beach make up this barrier island off the coast of Massachusetts near Newburyport. The natural vegetation includes heather, wild beach plums, and cranberries (there is a 3-quart limit per person in the fall harvest season). Geese and pheasant are only two of the bird species for watching. *FYI:* Write to the Refuge Manager, Parker River National Wildlife Refuge, Northern Boulevard, Plum Island, Newburyport, MA 01950; 508-465-5753.

Wachusett Meadow Wildlife Sanctuary, Mass.: This 1,000-acre park includes ten miles of hiking trails where many varieties of birds are visible to those who visit. *FYI:* Near Princeton; 508-464-2712.

Barre-Montpelier Region, Vt.: Bird species common to the Green Mountains and nearby foothills can be seen in this area. In Barre, the Thurman W. Dix Reservoir is a good place to watch migratory grebes and loons. *FYI:* Central Vermont Audubon Society, P.O Box 1112, Montpelier, VT 05602.

National and State Treasures

The parks featured here represent only a sampling of New England's national parks, state parks, and monuments. *FYI:* For a complete listing, write to North Atlantic Region, N.P.S., 15 State Street, Boston, MA; 617-223-5200.

Button Bay State Park and Lake Champlain, Vt.

Vt. Travel Division

Acadia National Park, Maine: Spread out over Mount Desert Island, Schoodic Peninsula, and tiny offshore islands, Acadia National Park offers visitors the chance to explore 120 miles of unspoiled trails, Somes Sound, the only fjord on the East Coast, and vistas from Cadillac Mountain (at 1,530 feet, it is the highest point along the Atlantic Coast north of Brazil). Visitors can rough it in one of the two park-administered campgrounds or take advantage of the nearby tourist accommodations in Bar Harbor. Popular activities in the summer include fishing, hiking, biking, and both lake and ocean swimming. Winter activities include cross-country skiing, snow-mobiling, and ice fishing. The Abbe Museum at Sieur de Monts Spring exhibits Native American artifacts from before the time of Champlain and the French and then English settlers. Bird-watchers may add some of the more than 300 species of birds to their life lists. *FYI:* Superintendent, Acadia National Park, Bar Harbor, ME 04609.

Baxter State Park, Maine: This outstanding state park was named for Perceval Proctor Baxter who deeded the land to the citizens of Maine on the condition that it be preserved "forever in its natural state." Mr. Baxter would most likely not be disappointed if he returned today; the park is primarily a wildlife sanctuary, and Mount Katahdin rises impressively from its heart. Don't look for motels, curio shops, or paved roads until you leave park boundaries. The best attractions are off-road, and Baxter's 160-mile trail system includes a portion of the Appalachian Trail. Mount Katahdin has been the subject of many Native American stories; Baxter Peak, Hamlin Peak, Pamola Peak, and South Peak are its highest summits. When Katahdin is viewed from an eastern vantage point, its Great Basin—carved by glaciers—is a striking feature. Hiking is possible throughout the year, but camping is seasonal and by reservation only. *FYI:* Baxter Park Headquarters, 64 Balsam Drive, Millinocket, ME 04462.

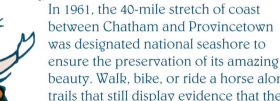

Cape Cod National Seashore, Mass.: In 1961, the 40-mile stretch of coast between Chatham and Provincetown was designated national seashore to ensure the preservation of its amazing beauty. Walk, bike, or ride a horse along trails that still display evidence that the Cape is a constantly changing glacial deposit. Swim on one of the six beaches, or visit the spot, near Provincetown, where the Pilgrims first landed before sailing on to Plymouth. *FYI:* 508-349-3785.

Monadnock State Park, N.H.: Follow in the footsteps of Ralph Waldo Emerson and Henry David Thoreau and climb to the 3,165-foot summit of Mount Monadnock. (This is one of the world's most frequently hiked peaks.) While you're at the top, it's interesting to note that early nineteenth-century farmers were responsible for the deforestation of your immediate surroundings. *FYI:* N.H. Division of Parks and Recreation, Box 856, Concord, NH 03301; 603-271-3254.

Odiorne Point State Park, N.H.: In 1623, Scottish fishing boats anchored here; it was the beginning of the first European settlement in the state. Today, visitors enjoy 137 acres of protected shoreline within this state park. Interpretive programs, picnics, and boating are popular activities. Boat launch. *FYI:* 603-436-7406; Rye.

Weather the Weather

Warm, humid air from the American Southeast meets cool, dry Canadian air and the result is the varied climate and unpredictable weather of New England. The four things you can count on are the seasons.

Spring: This season usually starts late and ends early; a fortnight of real spring weather is the exception. Snow melt can make navigating country roads a challenge due to plentiful mud. On the plus side, the tourist trade lightens, but beware seasonal closings as businesses and their owners prepare for the summer onslaught.

Summer: Expect it to be warm and humid, and you probably won't be disappointed. Anywhere from 70- to 90-degree daytime highs are the norm by mid-June, and it seems hotter because

Summer in Vermont

New England is a mecca for winter sports fans

of the moisture. Beaches, mountains, and interior lakes provide a cooling influence this time of year. This is the best time to go sailing along the coast or hiking in high country.

Fall: This is the season of sunny days, cool nights, and fall foliage. It is also the time of year when visitors flock to the area to watch the colors change. Sometimes the cooling trend in late September is followed by October's Indian Summer. This is also harvest time, and pick-your-own berries and other fruits are plentiful and sugar-rich.

Winter: Cold is the theme this time of year: minus 10 degrees is not uncommon, and annual snowfall in the mountains is around 100 inches. If you don't like the white stuff, head south and save New England for other seasons. Ski reports are broadcast on radio and television at regular intervals, and they also appear in print media. Special ski-condition phone reports are also in operation at peak ski season.

Annual Precipitation: 42 inches.

N.H. Office of Tourism & Travel Development

A cog railway climbs to the top of Mt. Washington, N.H.

Braving Mount Washington

New England's highest peak, Mount Washington, is part of the Presidential Range. The 6,288-foot peak is known for its atrocious weather. In fact, it's so bad, it inspires New Englanders to boast. Ice, bitter cold, snow, and fog—horror stories abound—and the mountain's weather is comparable to a subarctic climate. Just so you'll know, the record wind speed was clocked at a whizzing 231 miles per hour on April 12, 1934; the summit is fogbound a good 300 days per year. Now that you're inspired, head for the mountaintop via the 3½-mile Mount Washington Cog Railway, built in 1869 (it runs from May through Columbus Day), the auto road, or hiking trails. All routes are subject to closure when the weather is really bad.

GOING TO TOWN

Connecticut

Area: 5,009 sq. miles   **Capital:** Hartford

Pop.: 3,233,130   **Nickname:** Constitution State

C onnecticut" is a Native American word that translates loosely as "beside the long tidal river." Indeed, the Connecticut River divides the state roughly in half. Numerous colonial villages contrast sharply with heavily populated metropolitan areas such as Hartford, New Haven, Bridgeport, Stamford, and Stratford. Stretches of sandy beach and the historic whaling ports of Mystic, Stonington, and New London draw visitors to the shores of Long Island Sound. The Constitution State boasts an abundance of woodlands, state forests, and state parks. The exquisite Litchfield Hills extend from the Berkshire Hills and the Green Mountains.

Conn. Dept. of Economic Development

Hartford's gold-domed capitol has been the seat of state government since 1879

Hartford

Pop.: 131,299

Noted for: Wadsworth Atheneum, Mark Twain and Harriet Beecher Stowe houses, the Old State House, Center Church and Ancient Burying Ground, Bushnell Park, Constitution Plaza, Travelers Tower

Nearby: Noah Webster House and Museum in West Hartford, the colonial town of Old Wethersfield, Dinosaur State Park, New England Air Museum at Bradley Airport, Talcott Mountain State Park

Visitor's Information: 203-522-6766

Timber, animal furs, and sea access inspired Dutch traders to establish a post at the present site of Hartford in 1633. By 1636, the city had been founded by a group of Puritans, including the Rev. Thomas Hooker, who left the Massachusetts Bay Colony after a disagreement over strict Puritan dogma. At the same time, settlements were established in Windsor and Weathersfield. Together, in 1639, these three towns adopted the Fundamental Orders of Connecticut. Hooker was among those who drafted the New World's first constitution; hence, Connecticut is known as "The Constitution State."

Location and a wealth of natural resources ensured Hartford's role in the region's economic, social, and political growth. In 1662, the Royal Charter was drafted; it guaranteed the independence of the colonies of Hartford and New Haven. In 1687, Royal Governor Sir Edmund Andros demanded that the charter be revoked. It is believed that John Wadsworth, one of Hartford's patriots, hid the charter in the trunk of a great old oak. In 1688, the charter was reinstated. The oak was uprooted during a storm in 1856, and a plaque marks the spot where it once stood. Visitors to the city's museums will see various objects reportedly made from the tree's wood.

Conn. Dept. of Economic Development

Yale University, in New Haven, is one of the nation's oldest and most prestigious institutions of higher learning

Hartford's insurance industry dates back to the eighteenth century and the risky business of shipping. Today, modern office complexes house more than forty insurance companies.

Mystic

Pop.: 3,216
Noted for: Mystic Seaport, tall ships, Children's Museum, Marine Life Aquarium
Nearby: Stonington, a quaint coastal village where the lighthouse affords a view of three states
Visitor's Information: 203-536-1641

One of the top attractions in New England, Mystic Seaport is a restored nineteenth-century waterfront settlement. Three fully rigged sailing ships are moored in the harbor. Waterfront streets are lined with a nineteenth-century ship's chandlery, a tavern, a printer's shop, and various establishments offering hand-crafted goods. Visitors can board *The Morgan,* the last surviving wooden whaling ship in the nation. At the Children's Museum, kids can dress up in period clothing and learn games from the 1800s.

Maine

Area: 33, 215 sq. miles   **Capital:** Augusta
Pop.: 1, 205, 621   **Nickname:** Pine Tree State

The Vikings explored Maine's coastal region in the eleventh century; they found the area already settled by Native Americans. During the seventeenth century, the area was the site of constant battles between French and English claimants. In 1677, the Massachusetts Colony purchased Maine from a descendant of Sir Ferdinando Gorges, the British "Lord of New England." Maine became a state in 1820. Today, paper mills, lobstering, agriculture, and recreation-related businesses form the state's economic base.

The State House, Augusta

Augusta

Pop.: 21, 029
Noted for: Maine State Museum, Fort Western Museum, the State House
Nearby: Camden, Bath
The Pilgrims established a trading post on the east bank of the Kennebec River in the early seven-teenth century. Since then, Augusta's growth and prosperity can be attributed to the nearby woodlands and river commerce.

Bar Harbor
Pop.: 4,145
Noted for: Beaches, lobster, Acadia National Park
Nearby: Nova Scotia; a ferry is located one mile outside of Bar Harbor
Visitor's Information: 207-288-5103

Prominent American families such as the Rockefellers, Astors, and Vanderbilts built their summer mansions here in the nineteenth and early twentieth centuries. Unfortunately, a fire in 1947 destroyed many of these stately homes, but Bar Harbor remains a summer tourist center offering a variety of accommo-dations, fine shops, and restaurants as well as access to Acadia National Park.

Maine Office of Tourism

Bath

Pop.: 10,688
Noted for: Maine Maritime Museum, Bath Iron Works, colonial and Federal homes
Nearby: Popham Beach State Park
Visitor's Information: 207-443-9751

Bath was the nation's fifth-busiest port during the nineteenth century; Today, the 10-acre Maritime Museum Complex preserves the city's history of building some of the largest schooners of the period. The museum also offers a boat-building apprentice program and features an exhibit of Bath's 200-year-old lobster industry.

Boats in the Rockland Harbor

Maine Office of Tourism

Camden

Pop.: 4,468
Noted for: Camden Hills State Park, Penobscot Bay, Windjammer fleet, Laite Memorial Park and Beach
Nearby: Rockport, a quaint seaside town, and Vinalhaven Island, popular with vacationers
Visitor's Information: 207-236-4404

One of Maine's loveliest towns, Camden inspired resident Edna St. Vincent Millay to write her first poems in 1917. Several schooners may be boarded for windjammer tours of Penobscot Bay and the Maine seacoast.

Portland

Pop.: 61,284
Noted for: Its status as the state's largest metro area, Casco Bay, Portland Museum of Art, Old Port Exchange, Victoria Mansion, headquarters of the Victoria Society of Maine, Wadsworth-Longfellow house
Nearby: Casco Bay Islands, Calendar Islands, Sebago Lake and State Park, Cape Elizabeth, Freeport (home of L.L. Bean).
Visitor's Information: 207-772-5800

Portland began as a seventeenth-century trading post, but it was abandoned because of frequent raids by local Indian tribes. Resettled in 1716, it was Maine's capital from 1820 to 1832. The Old Port Exchange, an Urban Renewal complex of offices, shops, and restaurants on the waterfront, was revitalized in the 1970s.

Massachusetts

Area: 8,093 sq. miles   **Capital:** Boston
Pop.: 5,889,502   **Nickname:** Bay State

The region's first European settlements were established in Massachusetts; Puritans founded Boston. Fishing and the whaling trade formed the state's economic foundation for 200 years. In the nineteenth century, Massachusetts made the shift from maritime commerce to industrialization. Today, education, research industries, commercial fishing, and recreation are all part of the Bay State's profile.

Boston

Pop.: 577,825
Noted for: Freedom Trail, symphony orchestra, Boston Pops, ballet, opera, Museum of Fine Arts, Isabella Stewart Gardner Museum, Boston Common, Back Bay, Beacon Hill, the waterfront, Government Center, the Emerald Necklace parks system, sailing on the Charles River, Celtics, Bruins, Red Sox, Boston Marathon, Harvard, Radcliffe, Brandeis, Boston University, Wellesley, and Tufts
Nearby: Cambridge, Lexington, Concord, Charleston (Bunker Hill), Brookline (Kennedy's home), Salem, Saugus Iron Works
Visitor's Information: 617-727-3201

Known as "the cradle of American Independence," the capital of Massachusetts can also be considered the hub of New England. A walk in almost any part of the city reveals important historic sites of revolutionary times. Today, Boston is an educational center, a cultural center, a professional sports team center, an arts center, and the home of the unique Filene's Basement department store.

Boston Common along Tremont Street, ca. 1920

Boston Public Library

Lexington

Pop.: 28,644
Noted for: The Lexington Green, Minute Man National Historical Park, Buckman Tavern, Ye Olde Burying Ground, Museum of Our National Heritage
Nearby: Boston, Concord, and Cambridge
Visitor's Information: 617-862-1450

On April 19, 1775, eight Minutemen were killed by British soldiers on

Lexington Green. Paul Revere alerted the patriots that British General Gage was sending troops to destroy the colonial weapons stockpile. The Minutemen gathered at Buckman Tavern to await the arrival of the enemy. John Hancock and Samuel Adams, the two rabble rousers most wanted by the British, hid at the Hancock-Clark House, 36 Hancock Street, now restored.

Martha's Vineyard
Pop.: 9,540
Noted for: Beaches, sailing, whaling museums, Dukes County Historical Society, Gay Head Cliffs, Felix Neck and Cedar Tree Neck wildlife preserves, Manuel F. Correllus State Forest, Massachusetts State Lobster Hatchery
Nearby: Cape Cod
Visitor's Information: 508-693-0085

In 1602, mariner Bartholomew Gasnold christened Martha's Vineyard in honor of his daughter and the abundance of wild grapes he found there. Today, the town has a Victorian flavor, imparted mostly by the restored eighteenth- and nineteenth-century homes. Rent a bike and peddle the paths connecting the towns of Vineyard Haven, Oak Bluffs, Edgartown, and West Tisbury. Explore the lobstering waterfront village of Menemsha. Rent a sailboat, or just relax on one of the many beaches. The peak tourist months are July and August.

Nantucket
Pop.: 6,631
Noted for: Beaches, whaling, chamber music concerts, antique stores, eighteenth- and nineteenth-century homes, Nantucket Historical Association, the Maria Mitchell Science Center
Nearby: 'Sconset (the local name for the village of Siasconset, fishing expeditions, sailboating, sea kayaking
Visitor's Information: 508-228-1700

Settled by English colonists in 1659, Nantucket became a major financial contributor to the American Revolution, thanks to the flourishing whaling industry. By the early 1800s, Nantucket was one of the world's foremost whaling towns.

New Hampshire

Area: 9,304 sq. miles
Pop.: 1, 085, 237
Capital: Concord
Nickname: Granite State

This state is a basic triangle—roughly 160 miles long and 90 miles across at its widest point. The western and northern regions are marked by the mountainous Appalachian Range system, while the low-lying southern area eases into the Atlantic Ocean. Concord, Manchester, Keene, and Nashua are the state's largest cities. Portsmouth, situated on New Hampshire's 18-mile coast, is the Granite State's only seaport. New Hampshire's state flower is the purple lilac.

Statehouse, Concord

N.H. Office of Travel & Tourism Development

Concord

Pop.: 34,609
Noted for: The State House (built in 1819, the oldest state capitol in the U.S. still in use), Franklin Pierce Mansion (home of the fourteenth president), League of New Hampshire Craftsmen, exhibition and sale of glass, silver, and textiles

A covered bridge near Albany, N.H.

N.H. Office of Travel & Tourism Development

Nearby: Canterbury Shaker Village (restored 1792 settlement), Hopkinton antiques center, Lake Winnipesaukee (summer beaches and winter skiing)
Visitor's Information: 603-224-2508

First settled in 1725, Concord became the state capital in 1808, boasting the largest state legislature in the country, with 424 representatives. In the nineteenth century, the Abbot-Downing Company perfected the Concord coach, credited with settling the West because of its riding comfort. Although Concord produces granite, electrical equipment, and leather goods, it retains a rustic look and feeling.

New London

Pop.: 27,869

Noted for: U.S. Coast Guard Academy, Thames River, Joshua Hempstead House built in 1678, Whale Oil Row, Ye Ancientist Burial Ground, the Monte Cristo Cottage (the boyhood home of Eugene O'Neill)

Nearby: Mystic, Groton (the home of the U.S. Atlantic submarine fleet), Ocean Park beach and amusement park, ferries to Block Island, Fishers Island and Orient Point, Eugene O'Neill Theater Center—home of the National Playwrights Conference and the National Theater Institute

Visitor's Information: 800-863-6569/203-444-2206

St. Pierre/N.H. Office of Travel & Tourism Development

Fall harvest

New London has always had strong ties to the sea. It served as an important Revolutionary War port as well as a whaling port in the mid-1800s. Today, it is the home of the Coast Guard Academy.

Portsmouth

Pop.: 25,734

Noted for: Its status as New Hampshire's only seaport, Strawberry Banke, ten acres of restored eighteenth-century buildings, Prescott Park on the waterfront, the John Paul Jones House

Nearby: The town of Exeter and Phillips Exeter Academy; Isles of Shoals; New Castle, known for its colonial homes

Visitor's Information: 603-436-1118

In 1623, a band of English settlers in search of fertile land and fresh water arrived on the banks of the Piscataqua River and renamed it Strawberry Banke because of the abundance of wild strawberries. Later, it was once again christened Portsmouth, because of its port site at the mouth of the river; Maritime commerce brought the city prosperity. The restoration of Strawberry Banke features buildings from 1695 to 1835 along with costumed craftspeople who produce period furniture, pottery, and wooden boats right before your eyes.

Rhode Island

Area: 1,214 sq. miles   **Capital:** Providence
Pop.: 992,694   **Nickname:** Ocean State

The Arcade, Providence

"Little Rhody," the nation's smallest state, is also the most densely populated. The first European colonists to reach Rhode Island were fleeing religious intolerance in Massachusetts. They found the area already populated by Wampanoag and Narragansett Indians, and relations were peaceful until King Philip's War (1675–1676). In the eighteenth century, Rhode Island's economy was based on the sea; Providence and Newport were major ports. Maritime traders amassed fortunes that were used to finance the state's textile industry, and by the mid-nineteenth century, Rhode Island was the nation's most industrialized state. Today, fishing off Block Island is world-renowned, and Newport is a resort mecca.

Providence

Pop.: 900,000 (metro region)
Noted for: College Hill, Brown University, Rhode Island School of Design (and Museum of Art), First Baptist Meeting House, Prospect Terrace Park, University Hall, the John Brown House, the Arcase (a nineteenth-century mall with fine shops), Artist's Row galleries on Thomas Street, Benefit Street's restored eighteenth- and nineteenth-century houses, textiles, boatbuilding, jewelry manufacturing
Nearby: Charles E. Smith Greenhouses featuring a zoo, museum of natural history, lakes, and hiking paths; Pawtuxet exhibits of nineteenth-century water-powered textile production, including Slater Mill Historic Site; Saunderstown; Wickford, a restored colonial village
Visitor's Information: 401-274-1636

It is fitting that Providence declared Rhode Island to be independent of England in May 1776, two months before the American Declaration of Independence. Providence was founded by Roger Williams after he was banished from the Massachusetts Bay Colony for his anti-Puritan views on religion. Williams and a group of his followers ended their journey on the banks of the Moshassuck River, naming their settlement Providence because they felt that divine providence had led them there. Williams proclaimed that Providence would be a haven for all those seeking freedom of religion.

Providence changed from a farming economy to a shipping and trade center and served as an important supply depot during the Revolutionary War. Rhode Island College was renamed Brown University in 1804, in honor of its principal benefactor, Nicholas Brown II. Providence has preserved and restored many of its historic sites, making it a good walking city. The Providence Preservation Society offers self-guided tour booklets and audiocassettes.

Newport

Pop.: 27,704

Noted for: Mansions and historic homes and Cliff Walk, yachting, Newport Jazz Festival, Thames Street, Touro Synagogue, Quaker Meetinghouse, July Tennis Championships, Tennis Hall of Fame, Newport Art Museum, Fort Adams State Park

Cliff Walk, Newport

Nearby: Green Animals Topiary Gardens, the resort towns of Portsmouth and Middletown

Visitor's Information: 401-847-1600

Like Providence, Newport was founded by a dissenting settler, William Coddington, who split with the Puritan sect. As a result, Newport encouraged religious freedom by welcoming Quakers, Jews, and Baptists in the 1600s. During the revolution, Newport was occupied by British soldiers, which ended its port-based prosperity. However, in the late 1800s, the wealthy began building their summer mansions here. Take the Cliff Walk to visit the inside of Cornelius Vanderbilt's seventy-room mansion, the Breakers, built in 1885. Marble House (the home of William K. Vanderbilt), The Elms, and Rosecliff are also along Cliff Walk.

Vermont

Area: 9,614 sq. miles   **Capital:** Montpelier
Pop.: 562,758   **Nickname:** Green Mountain State

Pastoral view of E. Corinth

Vt. Travel Division

The Green Mountain State—"*les verts monts*," as explorer Samuel de Champlain exclaimed when he saw the state's wooded mountains—is distinguished by a landscape of hill and dale. This pastoral region has no major metropolitan or industrial centers, and the state's largest city, Burlington, has only 38,000 inhabitants.

Historically, Vermonters have been known for their spirit of independence. The area's earliest residents, Native Americans, fiercely defended their homeland against incursions by Europeans. Before the outbreak of the American Revolution, Ethan Allen and his Green Mountain Boys had captured Fort Ticonderoga from the British. Because of property disputes, the state opted for independent nation status for 14 years—Vermont minted its own money and negotiated with foreign powers—and did not join the union until 1791. The nineteenth-century dairy industry is still flourishing in Vermont; witness the famous Vermont cheddar.

Montpelier

Pop. 8,195
Noted for: Gold-leaf-domed Vermont State House modeled after Greek Temple of Theseus, Vermont State Museum, granite industry, Ben & Jerry's Ice Cream headquarters and tours
Nearby: Barre, Mount Mainsfield State Park and Mount Mansfield (Vermont's highest peak), the ski areas of Stowe and Sugarbush

With fewer than 9,000 residents, the charming, tree-filled city of Montpelier qualifies as the nation's smallest state capital. The Vermont State House you see today was built from the granite shell of its imposing predecessor, gutted by fire in 1857. The state's first capital structure, a nine-sided building, was built in 1808 and abandoned in 1836.

Barre

Pop.: 10,256
Noted for: Rock of Ages Quarry and tour, Hope Cemetery, statue of poet Robert Burns in City Park
Nearby: Active granite quarries, Brookfield and its floating bridge

Perched on the Winooski River in the Green Mountains, Barre has been the hub of the state's granite industry since the late nineteenth century, when the new railroad made transport feasible. In 1918, Italian craftsmen and stonecutters comprised half of Barre's population. Since 1900, French-Canadians have steadily resettled in this Catholic community, a rarity in Vermont.

Bennington

Pop.: 16,353
Noted for: Bennington College, Bennington Battle Monument, Old Bennington historic district, Old First Church, the Bennington Museum
Nearby: Woodford State Park with beach and over one hundred campsites, Molly Stark Trail and views of Massachusetts and New Hampshire

In 1777, the Battle of Bennington turned the tide of the Revolutionary War in the colonists' favor. Ethan Allen and the Green Mountain Boys rallied here in 1775 before capturing Fort Ticonderoga from British forces. (At the Bennington Battle Monument, take the elevators to the top of the 306-foot obelisk.) Today, this community is a blend of commercial, historic, and educational influences.

Burlington

Pop.: 37,125
Noted for: Champlain Shakespeare Festival, Vermont Mozart Festival, University of Vermont, Ethan Allen Park, Port Kent Ferry to New York
Nearby: Shelburne, Isle la Motte

Vt. Travel Division

A stroll in Burlington

Situated on Lake Champlain, Burlington is the state's largest city and its only urban and industrial center. Graceful residences are evidence of the town's successful history as a nineteenth-century commercial port. Today, corporations such as IBM and General Electric have revitalized the city.

TASTE OF NEW ENGLAND

Something Fishy

Conn. Dept. of Economic Development

Fishing boats and pleasure craft afloat in Stonington Harbor, Conn.

It's impossible to indulge yourself and your taste buds in New England without encountering freshwater and saltwater delicacies. Whether you take your food on the shell or the scale, there is much variety to choose from. For that, give credit where credit is due: the New England coastline stretches more than 2,000 miles along the Atlantic Ocean, and hundreds of lakes, ponds, and streams dot the inland countryside. Haddock, sole, flounder, pollack, cod, clams, lobster, bass, scrod, and trout are all common fare.

Most frequently, fish is filleted and then broiled, fried, or baked. Chowders and fish cakes—soft inside and crusty on the out-side—are also made from local fishes. Clams (a.k.a. "steamers" or "quahogs"), mussels, and scallops are found along the coast. New England clambakes originated with Native Americans. Charcoal fires were tended on the beach, rocks were heated and covered with sea-weed; clams, potatoes, and corn were layered over hot rocks, and another layer of seaweed topped off the pile. The distinctive flavor of the food comes from the combination steam-bake process.

New England Eats

Variety certainly is one spice of life, and New England's eats are nothing if not varied. Of course, that's to be expected in an area where so many cultures share the same territory.

In addition to fishes, crustaceans, and mollusks, hearty New England cuisine makes scrumptious use of pumpkin, squash, corn, and cranberries: all were growing here before

the first Europeans arrived. Native Americans instructed the first non-native settlers in the preparation of such foods. A traditional New England dessert is Indian pudding, a delicious concoction of cornmeal, molasses, milk, and spices. Fresh fruit pies in season topped with ice cream are also typical of the region. And don't forget maple syrup; it is hard to miss because bottles of the sweet are found on virtually every New England breakfast table.

Seafood in the Ocean State

R.I. Tourism Division

Food Festivals

Local festivals are a great way to sample regional food and to enjoy regional customs. The festivals listed below will get you started. Contact the Chamber of Commerce or Department of Tourism nearest your destination for more information on festivals and annual events.

→ Lobsterfest, Mystic, Conn., May
→ Ben & Jerry's One World One Heart Festival, Warren, Vt., June
→ Lobster Fest & Arts & Crafts Show, Niantic, Conn., July
→ Maine Lobster Festival, Rockland, Maine, Early August
→ Old-Fashioned Pie & Ice Cream Social, Ferrisburgh, Vt., August
→ Chowderfest, Old Orchard Beach, Maine, August

Food Trivia Quiz

1) Brown beans made with molasses and spiced with salted pork are known as ___c___.
   a) Providence baked beans **b)** Portland baked beans **c)** Boston baked beans
2) Johnny cake is made primarily with ___b___.
   a) whole wheat flour **b)** cornmeal **c)** maple syrup
3) Beef and vegetables boiled in a pot are called ___a___.
   a) New England boiled dinner **b)** stewmudgeon **c)** bangers and mash

ANSWERS: 1) c 2) b 3) a

Shell Game

Lobster is a major culinary item along the Maine and northern Massachusetts coasts. Traditionally, lobster is boiled and served with butter. Lobster bisque and lobster chowder, lobster salad, and lobster roll are all variations on the crustacean theme. They are incredibly delicious, but don't bite into a Maine or Massachusetts lobster lightly—this crustacean is a very interesting ocean dweller.

New England Golden Fish (or Lobster) Chowder

3 tablespoons butter	1 teaspoon salt
1 onion, chopped	¼ teaspoon pepper
1 stalk celery, chopped	1 bay leaf
3 tablespoons flour	¼ teaspoon thyme
5 cups milk	½ teaspoon dill
2 cups diced potatoes	2 cups shredded cheddar
(preboiled for 5 minutes)	cheese

1 pound fish fillets or 1 pound lobster (in pieces)

Melt butter in large saucepan. Add onion and celery and sauté until soft. Stir flour into butter mixture, simmer for one minute, and remove from heat. Pour milk slowly into butter/flour mix and stir. Return to low heat; simmer, do not boil. In separate pan combine preboiled potatoes and fish along with salt, pepper, bay leaf, thyme, and dill. Simmer 10 to 15 minutes. Add fish (or lobster) and potatoes to heated milk mixture; stir in cheddar cheese. Serve with toast or chowder crackers.

Reprinted with permission from Phoebe Phillips

American Lobster *(Homarus americanus)*

More than 500 million years ago, ancient crustaceans roamed the shallow seas. Today, modern crustaceans (such as lobsters, crabs, and shrimp) are very successful ocean dwellers. These armored animals depend on a tough exoskeleton made mostly of chitin for protection from

predators. In order for crustaceans to grow, the outer skeleton must be shed. This process is called molting, and it usually takes place once a year.

A molting crustacean crawls out of its old skeleton, and its soft body quickly expands before the new exoskeleton hardens over it. Molting takes hours, during which time crustaceans are very vulnerable to predators. They will often hide in a crevice or under a rock until their new armor has hardened.

A crustacean's armor is jointed, and the limbs come in "right-hand" and "left-hand" pairs. There are sections of flexible skin at the limb joints so the legs are movable.

To travel, lobsters walk on their eight legs or they swim slowly, using their legs and their swimmerets (abdominal appendages). They can also avoid danger with a quick thrust of the abdomen.

The American lobster lives in cold Atlantic waters off the New England coast and farther north.

Lobster Manners

1. Give the claws a twist

2. Crack the claws

3. Tear the tail from the body

4. Break flippers from tailpiece

5. Slide fork into opening where flippers used to be and push

6. Unhinge the back and look at the liver; it turns green when cooked

7. Crack the body open sideways to remove meat

8. Suck the meat out of small claws

Home Cookin'

Even when you're not at home, you can satisfy your craving for home cooking. The following recipes are included not only because they are now traditional New England fare, but because they're easy as well.

Barbecue Pork Ribs

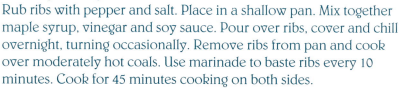

1 slab pork ribs (about 4 pounds)
1 teaspoon fresh cracked pepper
½ teaspoon salt
⅔ cup maple syrup
2 tablespoons rice wine vinegar
1 tablespoon soy sauce

Rub ribs with pepper and salt. Place in a shallow pan. Mix together maple syrup, vinegar and soy sauce. Pour over ribs, cover and chill overnight, turning occasionally. Remove ribs from pan and cook over moderately hot coals. Use marinade to baste ribs every 10 minutes. Cook for 45 minutes cooking on both sides.

Reprinted with permission from chef/author Jim Dodge, New England Culinary Institute, Montpelier, Vermont

Maple Crème Brulée

1 qt. heavy cream
10 egg yolks
⅓ cup pure Vermont
  maple syrup
1 vanilla bean
Heat cream with vanilla bean. Do not scald. Whisk pure Vermont maple syrup together with yolks. Whisk in some of the cream to temper. Add above mixture to cream and whisk. Pour into oven-proof baking cups and bake in water bath at 325° F/170° C until set, approximately 1 hour.

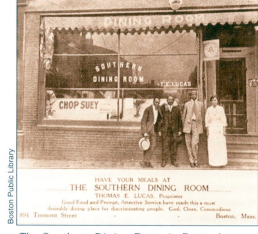

Boston Public Library

The Southern Dining Room in Boston's South End described itself as "Cool, Clean, Commodious"

Reprinted with permission from pastry chef Pat Oliver, New England Culinary Institute

Orange Cranberry Relish

Chop 2 cups (one bag) fresh cranberries and one orange in grinder. Add ½ cup honey. Mix together and store in refrigerator for at least two days before serving. Stir occasionally.

Reprinted with permission from The Vermont Beekeeper's Cookbook

Howard Karger/Mass. Office of Travel & Tourism

Early fall morning on a cranberry pond in Leverett, Mass.

Traditional Rabbit with Prunes in Anjou Fashion

1 4-lb. rabbit, disjointed	6 oz. small pitted prunes
¼ c. walnut oil	Salt, pepper to taste
1 medium onion, diced	1 tsp. sugar
3 medium carrots, diced	1 tied bundle of 3 sprigs of
Flour	thyme, 1 bay leaf,
½ c. white wine, Loire preferred	and 4 sprigs parsley

In frying pan, sauté the rabbit in the oil, then transfer to a covered casserole dish. Sauté the carrots and the onion in remaining oil and add to rabbit. Add flour and mix thoroughly. Drain fat from frying pan. Add wine and bring to a boil. Add ½ cup of water and the prunes. Add salt, pepper, sugar, and the bouquet of herbs. Cover and bring to a boil. Add pan mixture to contents of casserole dish. Bake in oven at 275° F for 1½-2 hours. Check for tenderness. Serve with egg noodles. Serves 6.

Reprinted with permission from Patrick Matecat, The Common Man Restaurant, Warren, Vt.

Sweet as Maple Syrup

Tapping maple trees the traditional way at Plainfield, Vt.

Vt. Travel Division

Sugar maples are synonymous with New England. In the fall, they produce splendid foliage, and year-round they yield delicious syrup made from their sap. As the sap begins to rise in the spring, a tube is inserted, and the dripping sap is collected. The sap is then boiled down into syrup. It takes at least 30 gallons of sap to equal 1 gallon of syrup.

Sugaring off occurs in the spring. Maine celebrates **Maine Maple Sunday** on the third Sunday in March. Sugarhouses statewide welcome visitors.

Parker's Maple Barn, N.H.: A century-old barn houses a restaurant, gift shop, and maple syrup house. *FYI:* Brookline Road, N.H.; 603-878-2308.

Fruits and Nuts

Although New England is known for its rocky, impoverished soil, subsistence farming was the mainstay of survival for many families until the mid-1800s. When farmers cleared their fields, the plentiful rocks were piled to create low stone walls—now a hallmark of the region. Between 1830 and 1860, more than 50 percent of the area was cultivated. But the move westward, toward more fertile lands, meant more and more of New England was reclaimed by wild vines, shrubs, and trees. Today, most of New England is forested; the 6 percent of the state that is cultivated for agriculture is planted with specialty crops such as blueberries and cranberries. The fruit stands and harvest festivals listed below are meant to provide just a taste of what is available.

Lyman Orchards, Conn.: Fields of vegetables and fruits are harvested here (there is also a golf course, restaurant, and farm market). *FYI:* Routes 147 and 157, Middlefield; 203-349-3673.

Strawberry Festivals, Conn.: Many small towns in the state host their own seasonal strawberry festivals during the month of June. *FYI:* First Congregational Church, Cheshire, and Town Green, Monroe.

Cranberry World Visitors' Center, Mass.: Everything you ever wanted to know about the esteemed cranberry. *FYI:* Water Street off Route 44; 508-747-2350.

Agricultural Fairs, N.H.: As various fruits and vegetables are harvested, the bounty is celebrated July through October. *FYI:* Stratham Fair, Stratham, in July; 603-431-GAME; Hopkinton State Fair, Contoocook, in September; 603-746-4191; or Sandwich Fair, Center Sandwich, in October; 603-284-7062.

Fall harvest, Hampden, Maine

Tom Hindman/Maine Office of Tourism

Allen Brothers, Vt.: This farm offers pick-your-own opportunities for strawberries and apples, in season. Sweet corn, apple cider, cheeses, and home-baked breads are also available for purchase. *FYI:* I-91, Exit 5, Vt.; 802-722-3395.

Strawberry Supper, Vt.: There are plenty of berries in various forms at this annual June event. *FYI:* Grange Hall, Dummerston; 802-354-6973.

Cheese Whiz!

Dairy farming is big business in New England. Vermont—noted for its big red barns—is the center of dairy land.

☛ **Crowley Cheese Factory, Vt.:** The state's oldest cheese factory, where visitors learn about cheesemaking the old-fashioned way. *FYI:* Route 103; 802-259-2340.

☛ **Plymouth Cheese Corporation:** Cheese, cheese, and more cheese. *FYI:* Off Route 100A; 802-672-3650.

Beverages and Brews

There are "dry" towns in New England: Vineyard Haven, Chilmark, and Gay Head on Martha's Vineyard, for instance. These are communities that don't allow the purchase or sale of alcoholic beverages. Although alcohol-free towns are the exception, nonalcoholic beverages are not. Maine's Poland Spring water is shipped nationwide, and plenty is consumed in the home state. The spring is situated near Rockland about three miles north of Sabbathday Lake. It became renowned in the 1800s when a seriously ill gentleman drank from the spring and recovered his health. A factory was soon bottling small quantities of the water, and a nearby spa catered to those who wanted to "take the waters."

Apple cider, freshly pressed, is an autumn specialty in New England. Cranberry juice, made from berries grown in the Massachusetts bogs, is used in fruit mixes.

When it comes to beer, Boston's premium **Samuel Adams lager** (and Schooner) is the pride of Massachusetts; it has also become extremely popular nationwide.

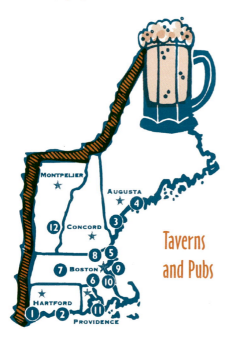

Taverns and Pubs

At the **Anheuser-Busch Brewery** in Merrimack, New Hampshire, visitors watch the brewing process in action, and samples are provided for those of legal age: 22 years old. *FYI:* 221 Daniel Webster Highway, N.H.; 603-889-6631.

Taverns, Pubs, and Other Drinking Establishments

Places of refreshment, good cheer, gossip, and historical import, New England's taverns are something special. The following list includes former taverns that are now museums, as well as working pubs and drinking establishments.

1) Keeler Tavern, Conn.: This establishment has been in operation since colonial days. Its nickname, the Cannonball House, comes from the cannonball that is stuck in the wall post—a reminder of the Battle of Ridgefield, April 17, 1777. *FYI:* 132 Main Street, Ridgefield.

2) Leffingwell Inn, Conn.: Political meetings were held here during the revolution. Today, the inn is restored and maintained as a museum. *FYI:* Norwich.

3) Jefferd's Tavern, Maine: Built in 1750, this tavern served as a way station on the York to Kennebunk stage route. The men congregated in the comfortable tap room, while the women and children stayed upstairs. *FYI:* Near the green, Colonial York.

4) Jed Prouty Tavern, Maine: Situated on the main street of this small town. *FYI:* Bucksport.

5) Buckman Tavern, Mass.: On April 18, 1775, Minutemen met at this pub in Lexington to await the British troops. After the battle, the wounded were given medical care under this roof. The tavern has been restored to its eighteenth-century appearance. *FYI:* Near the Green, Lexington.

6) Flynn's of Boston, Mass.: A fun place to eat, drink, and be merry. *FYI:* Massachusetts Avenue and Newbury Street.

7) Hall Tavern, Mass.: This museum dates to 1760. *FYI:* Historic Deerfield.

8) Lord Bunbury, Mass.: A prototypical English pub. *FYI:* North Quincy Market, Boston.

9) Monroe Tavern, Mass.: British troops were headquartered here on April 19, 1775 during the retreat from Concord . *FYI:* 1332 Massachusetts Avenue, Lexington.

10) The Sevens, Mass.: This is the real thing—a local, no frills, New England pub complete with dart board. *FYI:* Charles Street, Boston.

11) White Horse Tavern, R.I.: This one predates 1673 and claims the title of America's oldest operating tavern. *FYI:* Colonial Newport.

12) Old Tavern, Vt.: This lovely colonial building has been in business since 1801. Enter, and you follow in the footsteps of Rudyard Kipling, Daniel Webster, Woodrow Wilson, and Theodore Roosevelt. *FYI:* Colonial Grafton.

The Art of Viticulture

Roughly a thousand years ago, when Vikings surveyed the region, they called it "Vinland," probably because the countryside was tangled with luxuriant vines. Wild grapes were still thriving when Pilgrims landed at Plymouth 500 years later. Massachusetts' first governor, John Winthrop, tried to grow grapes from cuttings brought from Europe, but the vines died. The root aphid Phylloxera, aided by the region's severely cold winters, was probably what killed the European root stock.

Wineries

Over centuries, American vine varieties developed resistance to the deadly aphid, and settlers used native vines when *Vitis vinifera,* the European species, failed to flourish. By the early nineteenth century, growers had come up with sturdy hybrid varieties. But it was not until the 1970s and developments in cultivation of root stock that New England grape growing turned a profit. Today, New England wine-makers have made great strides in producing palatable wines.

1) Crosswoods Vineyard, Conn.: The winery is housed in a con-verted dairy barn near Stonington. *FYI:* 203-535-9174.

2) Haight Vineyards, Conn.: This beautiful winery in Chestnut Hill is an easy drive from Colonial Litchfield. New England apple wine and a variety of grape wines are features. Tours and tasting on the hour, year-round. You are welcome to picnic on the grounds and stroll the lovely vineyard walk. *FYI:* 203-567-4045.

3) Hopkins Vineyard, Conn.: Sweet to dry grape wines are offered here, as is hard apple cider. Tours are self-guided; call for specifics on tasting. There are picnic grounds at this New Preston winery. *FYI:* On Lake Waramaug; 203-868-7954.

4) Sow's Ear Winery, Maine: English-style dry rhubarb, choke-cherry, and apple cider wines are specialties at this fruit winery located near Blue Hill; visitors arrive by boat, car, or bus. Roads are bikeable but challenging. Seasonal tours and tasting. *FYI:* 207-326-4649.

5) Chatham Winery, Mass.: Grape, fruit, and flower wines (cactus flower wine and hibiscus flower wine, for starters) are created here. The winery's famous and unique lobster bottle won the National Glass Institute of America's Clear Choice Award in 1992. You will find both bottle and beverages for sale. In Chatham, tours are on Saturdays at 2:00 p.m., year-round. Tasting on a drop-in basis. *FYI:* 508-945-0300.

6) Chicama Vineyard, Mass.: The only winery on Martha's Vineyard was started in 1971 by George and Catherine Mathiesen, transplanted Californians. They feature roughly a dozen wines, including cabernets and zinfandels. Tasting and tours in the summer season; tasting only in the winter holiday season. *FYI:* 508-693-0309.

7) Nashoba Valley Winery, Mass.: This winery in Bolton (near Concord) offers wine tasting and guided tours (for a small fee), as well as pick-your-own apples and press-your-own cider (in season). *FYI:* 508-779-5521.

8) Plymouth Colony Winery, Mass.: The original cranberry wine is the specialty here. They feature a variety of fruit and grape wines. In Plymouth; seasonal tours and tasting. *FYI:* 508-747-3334.

9) Westport Rivers Vineyard and Winery, Mass.: Delicious wine tasting in a pastoral setting. Bring a picnic and relax. In Westport, this is also a good stop for bicyclists on local country roads. *FYI:* 508-636-3423.

10) Sakonnet Vineyard, R.I.: Founded in 1975, this was the state's first winery since Prohibition, but not the last. *FYI:* 401-635-8486.

11) North River Winery, Vt.: This Jacksonville winery is located roughly between Brattleboro and Bennington. There are 11 wines to choose from. You can make your selection when you taste and tour. *FYI:* 802-368-7557.

STATE OF THE ARTS

Jazz Fest, Maine

Cultural Events

New England's metropolitan areas enjoy distinct cultural seasons that include chamber music, ballet, theater, and symphony and other musical performances. The famous Maestro Seiji Ozawa conducts the Boston Symphony Orchestra; in the summer the orchestra plays at the Tanglewood Music Festival, near Lenox, in the Massachusetts Berkshires. More than 300,000 music devotees gather for the nation's most famous music fest. The Boston Pops is known for its outdoor concerts on Boston's Esplanade. And the well known Marlboro Music Festival is held each summer in Marlboro, Vermont.

Among the major theater events of the region is the festival sponsored by Williams College, in Williamstown, Massachusetts. Shakespearean theater is the specialty at the Mount, in Lenox, where novelist Edith Wharton once spent her summers.

Ballet, jazz, modern, and mime performances are regular events in various metro areas, but you can see them all at the renowned Jacob's Pillow Dance Festival held each summer in the Massachusetts Berkshires.

Bread Loaf Writers' Conference

Each summer, usually in late August, more than 200 writers from around the world gather at Middlebury College to attend the prestigious Bread Loaf Writers' Conference. The conference had its beginning in 1926; although poet Robert Frost played a part in its creation, John Farrar was the founding director. Writers of fiction, nonfiction, and poetry may attend. Acceptance is based on an application process that includes submission of a writing sample. *FYI:* Bread Loaf Writers' Conference, Middlebury College, Middlebury, VT 05753.

Festivals and Cultural Centers
Connecticut

Long Wharf Theater, 222
Sargent Drive, New Haven;
203-787-4282.

Shubert Performing Arts
Center, 247 College Street,
New Haven; 203-787-4282.

Yale Repertory Theater, 1120
Chapel Street, New Haven;
203-432-1234.

A Vermonter entertains the crowds
at Craftsbury festival

New Haven Symphony
Orchestra, Woolsey Hall, Yale
University, New Haven; 203-776-1444.

New Haven Jazz Festival, July, New Haven; 203-787-8027.

Maine

Bar Harbor Music Festival, July, Bar Harbor; 207-288-5103.

Massachusetts

Tanglewood Music Festival, July and August, the Berkshires; 413-637-1600, 617-266-1492.

South Mountain Concert Festival, summer and fall, the Berkshires; 413-442-2106.

Jacob's Pillow Dance Festival, July, Beckett; 413-243-0745.

Harborfest (and the Boston Pops Fourth of July Concert), July, Boston; 617-536-4100.

Berkshire Theater Festival, Stockbridge; 413-298-5576.

Williamstown Theater, Williamstown; 413-597-3400.

New Hampshire

New Hampshire Philharmonic Holiday Concert, December, Concord City, December; 603-647-6476.

Beauty of the Nutcracker Suite performed by the Nashua Symphony Orchestra and the Nashua Ballet Company, December, Nashua; 603-882-6221.

Rhode Island

Newport Folk Festival and JVC Jazz Festival, July and August, Newport; 401-331-2211 or 401-847-3700.

Vermont

Marlboro Music Festival, July and August, Marlboro; 802-254-2394.

National Traditional Old-Time Fiddler's Contest, September, Barre; 802-229-5711.

Fine Arts and Fine Artists

1) Wadsworth Atheneum, Conn.: An original 1842 Gothic Revival building houses the library and art gallery. Subsequent additions have made space for the extensive collection, which includes colonial American furnishings, seventh- through nineteenth-century European paintings, and American art from the colonial period to the present. *FYI:* 600 Main Street, Hartford.

2) Yale Center for British Art, Conn.: Elizabethan artworks include paintings from 1700 to 1850. Nineteenth- and twentieth-century British paintings and sculptures are also on view, as are sixteenth- and seventeenth-century works. *FYI:* 1080 Chapel Street, New Haven.

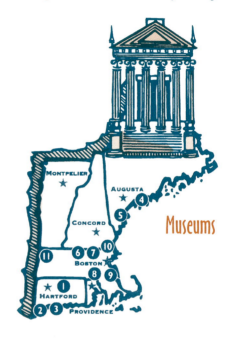

Museums

3) Yale University Art Gallery, Conn.: Ancient arts, nineteenth-century paintings, African arts, and Asian arts are all on exhibit here. The gallery was established in 1832 when artist John Trumbull donated 100 works. *FYI:* 1111 Chapel Street, New Haven.

4) William A. Farnsworth Library and Art Museum, Maine: The collection of nineteenth- and twentieth-century American watercolors and oils includes works by Andrew Wyeth and Winslow Homer. *FYI:* 19 Elm Street, Rockland.

5) Portland Museum of Art, Maine: Founded in 1882, this is Maine's largest public museum. Several additions have been added to the original McLellan-Sweat House including the Charles Shipman Payson building designed by Henry Cobb of I. M. Pei. Collections include nineteenth- and twentieth-century American art, in particular, works by Winslow Homer, Edward Hopper, and Andrew Wyeth. *FYI:* 7 Congress Square, Portland.

6) Busch-Reisinger Museum, Mass.: Noted for the work of twentieth-century German expressionists. *FYI:* Adolphus Busch Hall, Harvard University, Cambridge.

7) Fogg Art Museum, Mass.: This museum specializes in Western art from the Middle Ages to contemporary, with special focus on Italian Renaissance painting, impressionist painting and sculpture, and classical art. *FYI:* 32 Quincy Street, Harvard University, Cambridge.

8) Isabella Stewart Gardner Museum, Mass.: Paintings, sculptures, textiles, and furnishings make up the core of this collection. Isabella Stewart became a proper Bostonian on her marriage to Jack Lowell Gardner, but her vivacious personality ensured censorship from the establishment. This did not stop Isabella from creating Fenway Court to hold her extensive art collection. Flower gardens in the lovely courtyard enhance the experience. *FYI:* 280 The Fenway, Boston.

9) Museum of Fine Arts, Mass.: The art on exhibit was once in the private collections of wealthy nineteenth-century Bostonians. The Classical, Egyptian, Asian, and American art collections are impressive. The museum opened in 1876 in Boston's Copley Square. The need for space inspired new quarters designed by Guy Lowell in 1909 and by I. M. Pei and Partners in 1981. *FYI:* 465 Huntington Avenue, Boston.

10) Sackler Museum, Mass.: Asian art is the focus here. The collection includes Chinese bronzes and jades of special note. *FYI:* 485 Broadway, Harvard University, Cambridge.

11) Williamstown Sterling and Francine Clark Art Institute, Mass.: The Clarks gathered a collection of sculpture, paintings, and decorative arts that make it comparable to the world's finest museums. *FYI:* Williamstown.

Folk Arts

Vt. Travel Division

Northfield, Vt., Quilt Festival

In early New England, art and folk art were synonymous. All the necessities were made by hand, and each item was marked by the personality of its creator. Women were masters of the patchwork quilt: patches were pieced together or appliquéed. Sailors carved intricate scrimshaw on buttons, letter openers, forks, and knife handles to whittle away the long months on whaling vessels. Blacksmiths were often fine "smiths" in general; when the opportunity arose, they worked in silver and pewter. Shaker religious communities created tools, clothing, wooden boxes, chairs and other items of furniture. Today, folk arts and crafts are highly respected in New England.

Scrimshaw

Scrimshaw, the art of carving and etching ivory, especially whale teeth and jawbones, was practiced by sailors in the 1800s. The various steps involved in completing a work of scrimshaw were relatively simple, but the level of craftsmanship attained by many of the artists is still awe-inspiring.

1) The ivory was dried.
2) It was then polished and a design was etched with a knife or a needle.
3) Ink, tobacco juice, or soot was rubbed into the carving to add color.

Excellent examples of scrimshaw may be viewed at various whaling museums.

☞ **Kendall Whaling Museum, Mass.:** 27 Everett Street, Sharon; 617-784-5642.

☞ **Nantucket Whaling Museum, Mass.:** Broad Street, Nantucket; 508-228-1894.

☞ **New Bedford Whaling Museum, Mass.:** 18 Johnny Cake Hill, New Bedford; 508-997-0046.

Weather Vanes, Whirligigs, and Figureheads

The weather has never been easy to predict, but New England's farmers and sailors depended on carved wooden and cut metal weather vanes to predict change; the delightful aesthetic value of weather vanes was a by-product of utility. Christian symbols, fishes, horses, cows, whales, ships, and mermaids were all popular weather vane shapes. The wonderful grasshopper weather vane that tops the cupola of Faneuil Hall, Boston, was commissioned from Deacon Shem Downe in 1742.

Maine Office of Tourism

✱ *Shaker communities have traditionally produced everything they need to live. Their creations are valued by collectors for their functional and simple beauty.* **FYI:** *Canterbury Shaker Village, Canterbury Center (15 miles north of*

Whirligigs were a variation on the weather vane theme. These 3-D shapes were set into motion by the breezes, and they provided a good indication of wind velocity and direction. They also doubled as whimsical children's toys.

Ship carvers ran a regular trade carving figureheads, shop signs, and shop figures. The likeness of a shipowner's wife or daughters often adorned the prow of a whaling vessel, while anonymous windswept females adorned clipper ships. In lieu of television commercials, print ads, and billboards, the signs colorfully indicated the type of business represented. Many such signs can be seen at **Old Port Exchange**, a historic waterfront district in Portland, Maine.

Glass

Between the 1820s and the 1880s, famous Sandwich glass—pressed lacy glass—was factory-made and affordable. Although this new method of production made glass more available, methods of hand-blown glassmaking as well as cut and engraved pattern glassmaking were still in use. Collector-quality glass may now be seen at various New England glass museums.

☛ **New Bedford Glass Museum, Mass.:** Second Street, New Bedford; 508-990-0619.

☛ **Old Sturbridge Village Glass Exhibit, Mass.:** Sturbridge; 508-347-3362.

☛ **Sandwich Glass Museum, Mass.:** Sandwich; 508-888-0251.

☛ **Bennington Museum, Vt.:** Route 9, Bennington; 802-447-1571.

Artists' Studios

Educated at the École des Beaux Arts, J. Alden Weir went on to

Vt. Travel Division

Artist Terry Gregory at work

become one of America's leading Impressionist painters. The Connecticut farm that Weir purchased in 1882 became the inspiration for his paintings and those of other artists such as Childe Hassam, Albert Pinkham Ryder, and John Twachtman. Artists today still work in the house and studios, but visitors have the opportunity to stroll the grounds of the **Weir Farm National Historic Site**. *FYI:* 735 Nod Hill Road, Wilton, CT 06897; 203-834-1896.

American sculptor Saint Gaudens created the equestrian statue of General Sherman that guards the entrance to New York's Central Park. Gaudens executed most of his important work at the site of his home in Cornish, New Hampshire. The house, gardens, and studios in which he worked from 1885 until 1907 are open to the public at the **Saint Gaudens National Historic Site**. *FYI:* R.R. 2, Box 73, Cornish, NH 03745.

Art Colonies

By the turn of the century, a colony of artists and writers had gathered to live and work along Maine's rocky shoreline in the town of Ogunquit. Today, the **Ogunquit Art Center** exhibits the works of colony members. There are also several galleries and a small museum of art.

The **Provincetown Artists Colony** came into being at the turn of the century when artists and writers gathered here to work. Charles W. Hawthorne founded the **Cape Cod School of Art** in 1901, and Eugene O'Neill had his first play produced by the **Provincetown Players** in 1916 at the **Wharf Theatre**. John Dos Passos, Tennessee Williams, and Sinclair Lewis all worked and socialized in P-Town. Today, the town is still a cultural center.

Old Lyme is well known as an artist's colony, for the most part because Florence Griswold, a sea captain's daughter, had a penchant for art. Her house provided convenient room and board for many American artists in need of retreat. The **Lyme Art Association** stands next door, and many of the works completed in Griswold's home may be seen here. The **Florence Griswold Museum** has fine and decorative arts on display; there is also a gift shop.

Vt. Travel Division

Ceramic artist George Scatchard throws a bowl

Norman Rockwell (1894–1978)

Born in New York, Norman Rockwell moved to his home in Stockbridge, Massachusetts, in 1953. He demonstrated his artistic talent as a child and studied at the Art Students League. *The Saturday Evening Post* bought the first of 300 Rockwell covers when the artist was only 22 years old. His work chronicles day-to-day life in America. Roughly 200 drawings and paintings are part of the collection at the **Norman Rockwell Museum**. Rockwell's portrait of John F. Kennedy, his Stockbridge Main Street at Christmas, and the Four Freedoms are on view. *FYI:* Norman Rockwell Museum at the Old Corner House, Main Street, Stockbridge, Mass.; 413-298-4100.

Winslow Homer (1836–1910)

The landscape painter Winslow Homer was born in Boston. Although his career started with assignments as a magazine illustrator of Civil War scenes, Homer didn't begin painting full-time until he was forty years old. He is known for his realistic, intense, and very colorful style. He often worked at Prouts Neck, Maine, and the state's coast was his frequent subject. Homer is renowned for his naval and maritime oils and watercolors.

Literary New England

The New England landscape—its flatlands, seashores, oceans, and rolling hills—guides the shape the word takes on the page. It is there for the reader to see in the work of New England's literary luminaries. Herman Melville wrote Moby Dick while staying in Massachusetts, Henry David Thoreau had his cabin in Concord, poet Robert Lowell lived in Boston, and so did eighteenth-century African-American poet Phillis Wheatley. e.e. cummings was born in Cambridge, and Henry James once lived where the Harvard Faculty Club stands today. Edith Wharton's palazzo, The Mount, is located in Lenox. And Jack Kerouac has a park dedicated in his honor in Lowell, just north of Boston.

Nathaniel Hawthorne (1804–1864)

American short story writer and novelist, Nathaniel Hawthorne was born in Salem, Massachusetts, on July 4, 1864. Five generations of New England ancestors had included a judge in the Salem witch trials. Nathaniel's father was a merchant seaman who had risen to the rank of captain and whose travels included visits to Russia, India, and China. After her husband's death, Nathaniel's mother, Elizabeth Clarke Manning Hathorne (Nathaniel changed the spelling of his family name), moved next door to her relatives in Salem.

Boston Public Library

An introspective childhood left Nathaniel much time for reading. In 1821, he entered Bowdoin College (not far from Raymond, Massachusetts), and there he met Henry Wadsworth Longfellow. After his graduation in 1825, Nathaniel returned to Salem and spent his next years writing in solitude and publishing mostly anonymously and pseudonymously. In 1837, with publication of *Twice-Told Tales*, he emerged as the writer Hawthorne; within 15 years, he was known as a major American novelist. His published works include *The Scarlet Letter* (1850) and *The House of Seven Gables* (1851). *FYI:* The **House of Seven Gables**, Salem, Mass.; 508-744-0991.

Ralph Waldo Emerson (1803–1882)

Ralph Waldo Emerson—poet, philosopher, antitraditionalist, essayist, and definitive figure in American literature—was born in Boston on May 25, 1803. He was the fourth child of a distinguished New England family. Ruth and William Emerson ran a strict household based on the tenets of liberal Christian humanism. William Emerson died in 1811, and his son Ralph was strongly influenced by his aunt, Mary Moody Emerson, an aggressive intellectual involved in New Light Calvinism.

Boston Public Library

Emerson entered Harvard at age 14 to prepare for a career as a minister. His marriage to Ellen Tucker ended unhappily with her illness and death, and Emerson left the United States to tour Europe, where he met the major literary figures of his time. In 1833, Emerson returned to New England to begin a new career as essayist, poet, and lecturer.

For the rest of the decade, he associated with members of the Boston and Concord intellectual community, and he was one of the creators of the Transcendentalist movement. In 1837, Emerson met Henry David Thoreau, his Concord neighbor and his disciple, who helped found the Transcendental Club, a theologic and philosophic group. Emerson published his first work, *Nature*, in 1836. He was known as "the Sage of Concord."

FYI: The **Ralph Waldo Emerson House**, Concord, Mass.; 508-369-2236; **Walden Pond State Reservation**, Concord, Mass.; 508-369-3254.

Literary New England

Henry Wadsworth Longfellow (1807–1882)

Boston Public Library

Born in Portland, Maine, dramatist, poet, translator, and prose writer, Henry Wadsworth Longfellow was an institution in his own time. For 45 years, Longfellow lived in the house at Brattle Street, a short walk from Harvard Square, Cambridge. Here he wrote his poetry and with his wife, Fanny, entertained the luminaries of Boston literary society such as Nathaniel Hawthorne, Ralph Waldo Emerson, and William Dean Howells. Earlier, George and Martha Washington celebrated their seventeenth wedding anniversary in this same house, which the Washingtons inhabited during the siege of Boston in 1776. *FYI:* **Longfellow National Historic Site**, 105 Brattle Street, Cambridge, MA 02138; 617-876-4491.

Emily Dickinson (1830–1886)

Boston Public Library

Emily Dickinson, one of America's greatest poets, was born in Amherst, Massachusetts, into a family of ambitious males. Emily's grandfather, Samuel Fowler Dickinson, was one of the founders of Amherst College. Emily herself graduated from the Amherst Academy and spent one year at Mt. Holyoke Seminary, at which point she was more highly educated than most men of the era.

But the Dickinson family did not expect women to strive beyond a life of domestic interest; a published work by her father extolled the necessity of keeping females in their proper place. Emily Dickinson's role was to keep house for her father and then her own husband should she marry. Less than a dozen of her poems were published in her lifetime. After Emily's death in 1886, her sister Lavinia discovered roughly 2,000 poems among her papers. Many of Emily Dickinson's poems are concerned with the existential dilemmas of religious faith and mortality. *FYI:* There is a lovely garden at the **Emily Dickinson House**, Amherst; 413-542-8161.

Robert Lee Frost (1874–1963)

Robert Frost, the major American poet who wrote about rural New England, was born in San Francisco, California, in 1874. His father, a journalist who had left New Hampshire during the Civil War, died in 1885, and Frost's mother took the family home to live in New Hampshire and Massachusetts. Frost graduated from high school in Lawrence, Massachusetts, and entered Dartmouth College in 1892. After his withdrawal from school, he worked as a textile millworker and a schoolteacher before he entered Harvard in 1897. Once again, Frost did not complete college.

Boston Public Library

Instead, he moved to a farm in Derry, New Hampshire, where he and his wife lived for 12 years. The Frosts spent three years in London, where Robert established himself as a poet before he returned to New Hampshire. He sold his first poem in 1894. Frost taught at Amherst College, and he helped found the Bread Loaf School of English at Middlebury College.

Frost experienced tragedy in his life. His first child died of cholera, another died of fever, his daughter and his sister were committed to mental hospitals, and after his wife's death, his son committed suicide. Frost's numerous published works include *A Boy's Will*, *North of Boston*, and *New Hampshire*.

BUILDING NEW ENGLAND

From the Ground Up

Although New Englanders have a reputation for knowing their own mind, for more than two hundred years, Europe—via England—was the major influence on the human-made landscape. From the first colonial structures to Federal and Greek Revival style public buildings, European sensibilities were the first word.

Simplicity, homespun design, and wooden frame structures were the hallmarks of seventeenth-century American **colonial** buildings such as public meetinghouses, which played a crucial role in a town's political and religious life. **Old Ship Church**, in Hingham, Massachusetts—the last standing Puritan meetinghouse in the United States—dates to 1681, when it was constructed by ship's carpenters. The pulpit, box pews, and curved ceiling are all crafted of natural wood. *FYI:* 90 Main Street.

Plimouth Plantation, near Plymouth, Massachusetts, has excellent examples of early American colonial architecture. Homes, complete with chimneys, are framed by rough-hewn wood beams, floors are dirt, and roofs are thatched. Eventually, single-room dwellings evolved into two-story structures with a chimney-hugging stairway, wooden shingles, and a saltbox (lean-to) attached to the rear. **Hoxie House** (1637), in Sandwich, on Cape Cod, and **Whipple House** (1637), in Ipswich, on the north shore of Boston, are both examples of colonial style.

Cape Cod Style

Cape Cod style refers to the frame cottages built to withstand cape weather.

The **Friend's Meetinghouse**, in Newport, Rhode Island, was the regional center for the Quakers of New England. It was built by the Society of Friends in 1699. Note the stone supports, pulley-operated walls, and again, the "shippish" ceiling. *FYI:* 401-847-1600.

The **Joshua Hempsted House**, in New London, Connecticut, dates to 1678. This exceptional example of seventeenth-century architecture has walls insulated with seaweed, and the windows are leaded. *FYI:* 203-443-8332.

The **Buttolph-Williams House**, in Wethersfield, Connecticut, is a plain and simple American colonial home that was built in 1692. *FYI:* Broad and Marsh Streets.

John Winthrop, Jr., the son of the Massachusetts Bay Colony governor, journeyed to England in 1641 to recruit workers and shareholders for an iron-making venture in the New World. The result was the **Saugus Ironworks**, now a national historic site and reconstructed to its mid-1600s appearance. You can walk your way through the iron-making process of colonial times.

N.H. Office of Travel & Tourism Development

The John Paul Jones house in Portsmouth, N.H., is a lovely example of colonial architecture

Conn. Dept. of Economic Development

Litchfield Congregational Church dominates the village green of Colonial Litchfield, Conn.

The **Iron Works House**, which once served as the office and home of the manager of the Saugus Ironworks, is a fine example of seventeenth-century American Elizabethan architecture complete with gables, batten doors, and casement windows. *FYI:* 244 Central Street, Saugus, Mass.

Modern Architects
Philip Johnson, Louis Kahn, I. M. Pei, and Alvar Aalto are only a few of the modern architects whose work decorates Boston, Newburyport, Salem, Hartford, Portland, and other New England metropolitan centers. Boston's mirror-plated John Hancock Tower and Hartford's glass ellipse are both notables.

Georgian Style

Hand-in-hand with colonial prosperity came the desire for and the ability to afford the more ornate, harmonious styles inspired by the Italian Renaissance. Georgian architecture gains its name

The Georgian style Wentworth-Gardner home, Portsmouth, N.H.

Mike Rounds/N.H. Office of Travel & Tourism Development

from the three Georges who occupied the English throne from 1714 to 1820. A brick or wood facade capped with a low roof, updated classical proportions, and symmetry and balance were the elements of this style. Many building designs were inspired by the Palladian styles of English architects Christopher Wren and Inigo Jones.

Old South Church, Boston, is an example of a simple Georgian-style meetinghouse, while the **Baptist Church**, in Providence, Rhode Island, represents a much more elaborate model of this style.

Meander through the grounds of **Harvard University**, Cambridge, Massachusetts, to gaze at the brick, white cornice, and Palladian windows à la the Georgian style.

The Massachusetts town of Deerfield has fine examples of early Georgian homes. Of special note are the **Ashley House** (1733), the **Hawks House** (1743), and the **Dwight-Barnard House** (1754).

More Georgian

In almost all of New England, Georgian homes were popular up until the time of the revolution. Litchfield, Connecticut, was the exception; many of the homes you see there today were constructed or remodeled after 1780.

In Newport, Rhode Island, the **Touro Synagogue**, now a national historic site, was built in the Georgian style by Peter Harrison, who was also the architect of King's Chapel, Boston. Sephardic Jews from Spain and Portugal established Rhode Island's first Jewish community in 1658, but they would not have their own place of worship, the second oldest synagogue in the United States, until 1763. The design accommodates the graceful classical style to Sephardic ritual. The syna-gogue sits diagonally on the

Vt. Travel Division

The Old Round Church, Richmond, Vt.

street so that the Holy Ark inside faces east. Twelve Ionic columns rep-resenting the twelve tribes of Israel form the interior.

The **Brick Market**, also in Newport, was designed in 1761 by Peter Harrison. This is a clear example of the influence of the Palladian style on Georgian architecture. The market was the commercial center of Newport at the time.

The **Hamilton House**, close to Kittery, Maine, is a Georgian mansion complete with riverside gardens. The house was constructed in 1785 for a well-to-do merchant, Jonathan Hamilton, and it was the setting for nineteenth-century author Sarah Orne Jewett's novel, *The Tory Lover*. Note the building's carved cornices and archways.

Colonial style

(Incidentally, Sarah Orne Jewett (1849–1909) lived in a home in South Berwick, close to Kittery. In addi-tion to *The Tory Lover*, she wrote *Country of the Pointed Firs* and several other works.)

Federal Style

The popularity of the **Federal style** was ushered into post-revolutionary America when newly prosperous shipbuilders, merchants, and traders longed for imposing homes that would announce their status to the world. Large, square, but nevertheless delicate wood and brick buildings were usually unadorned except for columned

porches. Often, in seaports, federal style homes boasted a widow's walk where incoming and outgoing ships were easily viewed. Federal and Greek Revival homes can be seen in the coastal towns of Salem, Portsmouth, Nantucket, Providence, New Bedford, and Newburyport. Samuel McIntire of Salem and Charles Bulfinch of Boston were the prevailing Federal-style architects in New England.

The **State House** (the Massachusetts state capitol), on Beacon Hill, Boston, was designed by Charles Bulfinch.

College Hill, in Providence, Rhode Island, has many Federal homes to view.

Washington Square and **Chestnut Street**, both in Salem, Massachusetts, boast notable mansions designed in the Federal style, a clear statement of the prosperity of the town's residents in the early nineteenth century.

Sarah Hood/Mass. Office of Travel & Tourism

South Market at Faneuil Hall, downtown Boston

Fenway Court and Isabella Stewart Gardner

When Isabella Stewart married Jack Lowell Gardner in 1860, she joined the ranks of the proper Bostonians. Nevertheless, Mrs. Gardner continued to irritate Society with her strong, independent personality and lack of concern for external censorship. Isabella was a collector. Not only did she acquire a breathtaking stash of art treasures, but she also acquired people. Soon-to-be art expert Bernard Berenson met Isabella when he was still a Harvard undergraduate. Through the years, he directed many of her artistic acquisitions.

Isabella created the impressive Fenway Court, her "Eyetalian palace" to house her extensive art collection. True to her style, she told the building inspector, "If Fenway Court is to be built at all, it will be built as I wish and not as you wish." After years of construction—using stone lions from Florence, balconies from the Ca' d'Oro, the Venetian *palazzi*, and other bits and pieces of European palaces, monasteries, and houses—Fenway Court was unveiled at a 1903 New Year's Eve grand gala attended by everyone who was anyone in Boston.

Ca' d'Oro's Gothic balconies line the three-story covered courtyard of Fenway Court. Ornate and formal floral gardens are dotted with statues. A mosaic floor was taken from the Roman villa of the empress Livia. Do not miss an opportunity to view the building and the amazing art collection it still contains. *FYI:* The Fenway; 617-566-1401.

Greek Revival

Domes, columns capped with Ionic capitals, an optimistic style on a grand scale modeled after classical Greek temples—these are the hallmarks of the **Greek Revival style** of the 1800s. Public buildings were constructed of marble or granite, while domestic building materials varied.

Quincy Market (1825), the crux of the Faneuil Hall Marketplace in Boston, and the Providence **Arcade** (1828) are both examples of Greek Revival architecture.

Domestic architecture in the Greek Revival style may also be viewed in the lovely town of **Grafton, Vermont**.

Victorians

During the latter half of the nineteenth century, in the Victorian Era wealthy mill owners employed the architectural firm of McKim, Mead and White and Henry Hobson Richardson to design extravagant fancies based on Italian Renaissance architecture.

Pink House, Oak Bluffs, Mass.

Trinity Church, Copley Square, Boston, was designed by Henry Hobson Richardson, and it is in the style characteristic as Richardson Romanesque.

Wander around **Oak Bluffs**, Martha's Vineyard, and you'll see fine examples of Victorian gingerbread.

Justin Smith Morrill Homestead, Strafford, Vt.

Take the Cake

The towns of Kennebunk and Kennebunkport, Maine, boast many nineteenth-century homes and commercial buildings. Architectural walking tours are offered during the summer season. *FYI:* 207-967-0857.

Legend has it that the **Wedding Cake House** in Kennebunk, was inhabited by a captain who was married hurriedly before departing on a sea voyage. Because there had been no time for a true wedding cake, the captain had the house "frosted" for his bride when he returned. Although the Wedding Cake House is not open to the public, the gingerbread trim facade is worth an outside look. *FYI:* Route 9A, Kennebunk, Maine.

Mark Twain's Home

Mark Twain wrote, "But if you hurry a world or a house, you are nearly sure to find out, by and by, that you have left out a towhead, or a broom-closet, or some other little convenience, here and there, which has got to be supplied, no matter how much expense or vexation it may cost."

When Twain built his own home in a small literary community (already inhabited by Harriet Beecher Stowe and Charles Dudley Warner) known as Nook Farm in West

Conn. Dept. of Economic Development

Mark Twain's Victorian home at Nook Farm, in West Hartford, Conn., was designed by architect Edward Potter

Hartford, Connecticut, he took his time. Although traditional Hartford homes were square, boxy designs, Twain assured his architect, Edward Potter, that he would most definitely go against tradition. In 1874, the house on Farmington Avenue was completed at a cost of $125,000—paid for by a writer, no less! It emerged as a Victorian classic with porches, gables, balconies, chimneys, and verandas; it has been likened since to a Swiss cuckoo clock.

One porch was decorated as a steamboat pilot house reminiscent of life on the Mississippi River, a study overlooking the garden looked a bit like a Middle Eastern monastery, and a plant-strewn conservatory was designed to encourage the author's muse. But Twain chose to write many of his works in the billiard room. Although Twain attained great success and prospered for much of his life, financial troubles hit in the late 1880s, and by 1894, the writer was bankrupt. The Twain house was put up for sale in 1902. *FYI:* 351 Farmington Avenue, West Hartford, Conn.

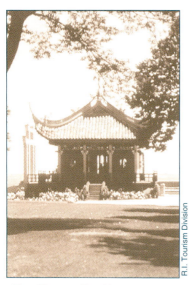

R.I. Tourism Division

The Chinese Tea House at Marble House, Newport

Newport, Rhode Island, and Its Buildings

The Revolutionary War, the War of 1812, and the hurricane of 1815 had a devastating effect on the culture and commerce of eighteenth- and early nineteenth-century Newport. Although attempts to revitalize the town industrially did not really succeed, Newport had three fine assets: location, location, and location. Sea air and beautiful surroundings lured vacationers until their numbers swelled in the mid-nineteenth century. Summer settlers built their own dwellings and resort structures, and by 1900, Newport was a veritable architectural oasis.

Newport's notable structures are the subject of very large books. Impeccable, charming, quaint, imposing, extravagant, and decadent are all adjectives that would apply to various homes and mansions. Styles represented include simple American colonial, Greek and Gothic Revival, Queen Anne, Federal, and American cottage. Although an estimated 480 buildings of one sort or another were destroyed during the Revolutionary War and the American blockade of Newport, the town is still an architectural historian's dream.

Hunter House National Historic Landmark was built in the late colonial style in 1748 by the deputy governor of Rhode Island, Jonathan Nichols. Today, you can still admire the furnishings, Townsend and Goddard, made in eighteenth-century Newport. *FYI:* 54 Washington Street.

Kingscote dates to 1839. It was built by Richard Upjohn for George Noble Jones. William Henry King, a China trade purveyor, gained ownership of the cottage in 1864. *FYI:* Bellevue Avenue.

Château-Sur-Mer is an extravagant Victorian home built in 1852 for William S. Wetmore, a China trade merchant. Richard Morris Hunt began major renovations in 1872. *FYI:* Bellevue Avenue.

Gilded Age Architecture

During the Gilded Age at the turn of the century, society (with a capital "S") occupied Newport "cottages" for a maximum period of two months each summer season. The rest of the time, the great mansions were cared for by servants and groundskeepers.

☛ **The Breakers**, a haughty and imposing mansion inspired by the Italian Renaissance, was designed by Richard Morris Hunt and built in 1895 for Cornelius Vanderbilt. It may remind you of a northern Italian palace—it was designed to do that. The grounds overlook the famous Cliff Walk. *FYI:* Ochre Point Avenue.

The Breakers, Newport

R.I. Tourism Division

☛ **Rosecliff**, a terra-cotta mansion, was designed by Stanford White and constructed in 1902 for Mrs. Hermann Oelrichs. Any resemblance to the Grand Trianon at Versailles? Ah, yes, it was planned that way. *FYI:* Bellevue Avenue.

☛ **Marble House**, the most splendid of the Newport cottages, was designed by Richard Morris Hunt and completed in 1892 for William K. Vanderbilt. The furnishings are all originals, and the grounds include a Chinese teahouse. *FYI:* Bellevue Avenue.

☛ **The Elms** dates to 1901 and was designed by architect Horace Trumbauer. Edward J. Berwind, a coal magnate from Pennsylvania, commissioned this home as a summer residence. The grounds are not to be missed. *FYI:* Bellevue Avenue.

☛ Built in 1880 as the East's most exclusive country club, **Newport Casino** honored the height of the Gilded Age. McKim, Mead and White designed the shingle style buildings, and the casino's grass courts were the location of the first Men's United States Lawn Tennis Association tournaments between 1881 and 1914. *FYI:* Bellevue Avenue.

Gardens and Greenery

Frederick Law Olmsted is the visionary who is credited with inventing the concept of the American city park. Believing that city folks have a need and a right to enjoy close proximity to nature, Olmsted, with his partner, architect Calvert Vaux, supervised the creation of New York's

Green Animals Topiary Gardens, Portsmouth, R.I.

R.I. Tourism Division

Central Park. Olmsted then moved to the Boston suburb of Brookline, setting up the world's first full-scale landscape architecture practice in a rambling farmhouse. Here, he designed Boston's five-mile park system, **The Emerald Necklace**. Visit Olmsted's house-office complex and grounds, then go on to the varied terrain of the Boston Park system he designed. *FYI:* 99 Warren Street, Brookline, MA 02146.

Built in 1681, the typical New England saltbox house at **133 Franklin Street** was the birthplace of John Adams, the second U.S. president. The city of Quincy along with the Adams Memorial Society donated this house and the adjacent house at 141 Franklin Street, which saw the birth of John and Abigail's son John Quincy, the nation's sixth president, to the people of the United States. Four Adams generations, including the two presidents, also lived at their farm, **Peacefield**, cultivating orchards and gardens that can be enjoyed today. Each summer, the white York rose that Abigail Adams originally brought from England and planted in 1788 still blooms. *FYI:* **Adams National Historic Site**, Quincy, Mass.; 617-773-1177.

The delightful and whimsical animal topiary gardens at **Green Animals**, in Portsmouth, Rhode Island, were started in 1880 by Thomas Brayton. More than eighty sculptured shrubs and trees, fruit and vegetable gardens, and flower beds create this green fantasyland. Visitors may also shop at the plant and gift shop or view the Victorian toy museum. *FYI:* Cory's Lane.

Park-McCullough House is a Victorian mansion complete with charming garden. *FYI:* Park and West streets, North Bennington, Vt.; 802-442-5441.

The historic homes associated with several Massachusetts writers have lovely gardens that are carefully maintained, and visitors are welcome. The **House of Seven Gables** in Salem has boxed flower and rose beds. **Emily Dickinson's House** in Amherst has gracefully sloping grounds planted with flowers and shrubs and great trees. Louisa May Alcott's father, Bronson Alcott, tried a brief experiment with communal living on a farm in Harvard, just west of Boston. After the experiment failed, Bronson moved back to **Orchard House**, on Lexington Road, Concord. The former **Fruitlands Farm** is now a museum situated on 200 lovely acres overlooking the Nashua River valley.

Gillette's Castle

William Gillette, the foremost English actor, played the part of Sherlock Holmes in 1899. The role brought him fame and prosperity; the money—more than $1 million—went into a 24-room castle overlooking the Connecticut River valley. The walls are four feet thick, and mechanical locking doors and furniture on moveable tracks added to the unique quality of the residence. A three-mile miniature railway carried guests around the grounds. In 1943, Connecticut purchased the land, which is now open to the public. *FYI:* Hadlyme, Conn.

Conn. Dept. of Economic Development

The unique castle residence of actor William Gillette is open to visitors to Hadlyme, Conn.

THE SPORTING LIFE

Be a Sport

New England has endless offerings for recreational pleasure. Those who prefer their leisure dry will not be disappointed. Hiking, biking, horseback riding, ballooning, bird-watching, camping—it's your call. If your athletic preference runs to aquatic environments you can indulge in snorkeling, canoeing, kayaking, fishing, scuba diving, or water-skiing. And for those who prefer to sit back and relax, festivals and racing and sporting events may fill your spectating bill.

Life's a Beach

The coast of New England is rugged, varied, and scenic. Maine alone boasts 2,400 convoluted coastal miles—only 228 miles as the crow flies. New Hampshire has 18 miles of beach-studded coastline, the Massachusetts shoreline covers 1,500 miles and includes Cape Cod National Seashore, while Rhode Island, the "Ocean State," boasts 400 shoreline miles.

1) Hammonasset Beach State Park, Conn.: This is the state's longest public beach. Quiet Long Island Sound waters make state beaches popular for families. *FYI:* Near Clinton; 203-245-1817.

2) Rocky Neck State Park, Conn.: This mile-long crescent beach is a good spot for swimming, hiking, fishing, camping, and picnicking. *FYI:* Route 156, Niantic; 203-739-5471.

3) Popham Beach State Park, Maine: The resort village of Popham Beach sits on the tip of a peninsula between

Beaches

the Kennebec River and the sea. It is the site of one of the earliest English New World settlements, established in 1607 at Popham Beach. Although the original colony survived only for a single year, diligent workers managed to complete the first ship built in America: the *Virginia*. Popham Beach State Park boasts a sandy beach on the peninsula's ocean boundary; day-use only. *FYI:* 16 miles south of Bath on Route 209.

4) Cape Cod National Seashore, Mass.: In 1961, federal legislation designated this area a national seashore in a campaign spearheaded by JFK. Nauset Light Beach (in Eastham) and Marconi Beach (in South Wellfleet) seem to go on forever. *FYI:* Salt Pond Visitor Center, Eastham; 508-255-3421.

5) Nantucket and Martha's Vineyard beaches, Mass.: These are popular resort beach islands. Families favor Jetties Beach and Dionis Beach, both on Nantucket, where the surf is lighter and lifeguards watch over things.

Kindra Clineff/Mass. Office of Travel & Tourism

Massachusetts Cape public beaches include Town Neck Beach, Sandwich, Point of Rocks Beach, Brewster, and Head of the Meadow Beach (pictured here), Truro. On the mainland, Horseneck Beach State Reservation, Westport, offers beachcombers hundreds of acres of white sand.

6) Hampton State Beach, N.H.: Miles of sandy beaches offer swimming and beachcombing opportunities. *FYI:* Route 1A, Hampton; 603-926-3784.

7) Kingston State Beach, N.H.: If you prefer a beach without salt, this southernmost freshwater park stretches along the northeast shore of Great Pond. You'll be close to the seaside, and the swimming is easy. *FYI:* Off Route 125 S., Kingston; 603-642-5471.

8) Block Island beaches, R.I.: This small island is a summer retreat for natives and visitors alike. The beaches are plentiful, and seasonal bird-watching adds feathered incentive for a visit. *FYI:* About 12 miles south of Point Judith; reachable via ferry from Galilee or Providence.

Wet Recreation

Whether your taste in water sports runs to swimming, water-ski-ing, sailing, or canoe-ing, you can satisfy your craving in New England. Parts of New England can be reached only by boat. That shouldn't stop you; if you don't own a watercraft, you can rent one.

Lakes & Rivers

1) Housatonic and Connecticut river states: Even beginners can canoe these rivers between Dalton and Great Barrington within the Acadia Wildlife Sanctuary. Whitewater river crafting is another way to see the sights along the Housatonic River, Connecticut.

2) Allagash Wilderness Waterway, Maine: This 92-mile wilderness waterway is heaven for experienced canoeists. Area facilities are primitive; don't look for telephones or public transportation. To enter the Allagash Waterway, visitors must register at the Umsaskis Lake or Michaud Farm checkpoints, at the Telos-Chamberlain entrance, or at Churchill Dam. *FYI:* Maine Bureau of Parks and Recreation, State House Station 22, Augusta, ME 04333.

3) Moosehead Lake, Maine: This remote lake is New England's largest: 120 square miles. Islands, coves, and bays are all part of the lake's outline. The surrounding forest is a popular hunting area. Fishing, canoeing, and rafting are all recreational possibilities. *FYI:* Greenville Chamber of Commerce; 207-695-2702.

4) Quabbin Reservoir, Mass.: The Swift River was dammed to create this great reservoir that serves the Boston area. The Native American word *quabbin* translates roughly as "a lot of water": the reservoir capacity exceeds 400 billion gallons. There were more than 50 islands created when the valley was flooded. Fishing, hiking, and picnicking are all popular activities. Swimming and hunting are pro-hibited. *FYI:* Via Route 9, 2 miles from Belchertown.

5) Lakes Region, N.H.: Lake Winnipesaukee, Squam Lake, and Lake Wentworth are among the more than 600 ponds and lakes that earn

Canoeing on Waterbury Reservoir, Waterbury, Vt.

Vt. Tourism Dept.

New Hampshire its nickname, "the Lakes Region." Deep-water lakes provide superior fishing and boating opportunities. The 72-square-mile Lake Winnipesaukee contains more than 270 habitable islands. Boating options include rentals, charters, and cruises; the Mt. Washington cruise departs from Weirs Beach. Lake trout and salmon are all best caught from boats. *FYI:* Lakes Region Association, P.O. Box 300, Wolfeboro, NH 03894; 603-569-1117.

6) Scituate Reservoir, R.I.: Boating, swimming, and fishing are all popular activities at this man-made lake. *FYI:* 401-272-1400.

7) Lake Champlain, Vt.: In 1609, Samuel de Champlain encountered this lake that qualifies—after the Great Lakes—as the nation's largest body of fresh water. Situated in a valley between the Adirondacks and the Green Mountains, the lake is a major recreation spot. Grand Isle, Isle la Motte, and North Hero Island may all be reached by bridges, and ferries cross between Vermont and New York. *FYI:* 802-863-3489.

The Charles

Just pass the sailing test at **Boston's Community Boating** (at the Esplanade), and you may rent a craft to tackle the Charles River, which separates Boston from Cambridge.

/our Feet!

Millions of acres of public land, much of which offers a full range of recreational opportunities, are there for the hiking in New England. Those listed below are only a sampling.

Baxter State Park, Maine: This 200,000-acre park is at the center of Maine's wilderness country. Mount Katahdin (5,267 feet at Baxter Peak), the highest point in the state, dominates the park, which is named for Perceval Proctor Baxter (1876-1969). The park is a wildlife sanctuary where visitors may glimpse deer, moose, and bear throughout the dense forest. Roads and camping facilities are primitive. The park's 160-mile trail system includes the northern branch of the Appalachian Trail. Trails are most numerous in the park's southern regions. To reach the top of Mount Katahdin, many fit visitors follow the 10½ mile Hunt Trail; the trailhead is located at Katahdin Stream Campground. *FYI:* Park headquarters are in Millinocket; reservations are required for campers; write: Reservation Clerk, Baxter Park Headquarters, 64 Balsam Drive, Millinocket, MA 04462.

White Mountain National Forest, N.H.: This national forest covers more than 760,000 acres of the White Mountain region, and it includes 650 miles of fishing streams as well as lakes and ponds. For hikers, 1,200 miles of foot trails—including the **Appalachian Trail**—traverse some of the tallest peaks in the East. The **Appalachian Mountain Club** (Pinkham Notch, Gorham, NH 03581; 603-466-2727) can give you information about places to hike and lodge along the portion of the trail contained in

Appalachian Trail
The Appalachian Trail runs more than 2,000 miles from Georgia to Maine. *FYI:* The Appalachian Trail Conference, P.O. Box 807, Harpers Ferry, WV 25425; Appalachian Mountain Club, 5 Joy Street, Boston, MA 02108; Pinkham Notch Camp, Gorham, NH 03581.

White Mountain National Forest.
FYI: Mt. Washington Valley Chamber of Commerce, Box 385S, North Conway, NH 03860; 603-356-3171 for general info about the region.
Green Mountain National Forest, Vt.: These mountains reach their greatest heights in Vermont,

Hikers ascending Camel's Hump, Vt.

where they provide the state's major recreation area. (Where the chain extends into Massachusetts, it is known as the Berkshires.) Downhill skiing is the winter sport here; hiking is the summer sport. The **Long Trail** follows the ridge of the Green Mountains. Weather conditions are subject to rapid change at high elevations; be sure you are fully advised as to weather, and carry enough water, food, bug repellent, and adequate clothing. *FYI:* 802-747-6700.

Campers enjoy White Mountain National Forest

Mt. Washington

Mt. Washington, at 6,288 feet, is the tallest peak in the White Mountain chain. Trails up the mountain vary from easy to tough; weather is subject to quicksilver changes. *FYI:* On trails and safety, contact the White Mountain National Forest, Forest Supervisor's Office, 719 Main Street, P.O. Box 638, Laconia, NH 03247; 603-528-8721.

Biking

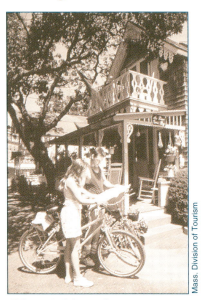
Mass. Division of Tourism

Biking in Massachusetts

New England is filled with back-country roads traversing soft rolling hills that seem to have been created with bikes in mind. You'll pass farmsteads, cornfields, fruit orchards, and villages. Pack a rain slicker and wear bright colors. On other bike trails, you can stay off roads and travel along beaches or follow old railroad routes. Observe bike safety regulations at all times.

☞ **Connecticut state parks and forests:** Bloomfield State Park at Penwood, Simsbury State Park at Stratton Brook, and Haddam State Forest at Cockaponset all maintain public biking trails. You can plan your excursions to accommodate bikers of all ages and levels. *FYI:* Bureau of Parks & Forests, Conn. Dept. of Environmental Protection, 165 Capitol Avenue, Hartford, CT 06106; 203-566-2305.

☞ **Cape Cod National Seashore, Mass.:** Numerous biking, hiking, and dune trails traverse this seashore. Marconi Beach (named for Italian physicist Guglielmo Marconi, who established the transatlantic wireless station here in 1901), Head of the Meadow Beach, Coast Guard Beach, and Nauset Light Beach lie within park boundaries. The 8-mile sandy trek to Great Island in Wellfleet is a smooth ride.

☞ **Cape Cod Rail Trail, Mass.:** The bike path travels the old railroad bed between Boston and Provincetown. Start your excursion at Route 134 in Dennis and peddle for 20 miles. Be sure to bring your swimsuit, because this trail stops at Coast Guard Beach in Eastham.

☞ **Martha's Vineyard and Nantucket, Mass.:** Level roads and trails include the 10-mile route from Oak Bluffs through Edgartown to Katama Beach, Martha's Vineyard, as well as the 5-mile Madaket bike trail to the west side of Nantucket and the 7-mile Siasconset path on the island's east flank. Rent a bike or carry your own on the ferry.

☞ **Mohawk Trail, Mass.:** Spectacular fall foliage and scenic views make this stretch of highway in the northwest corner of the state a popular route. The athletically inclined may bicycle through tiny villages and sheer river gorges and over covered bridges. This was once an Indian trail that traversed the banks of the Cold and Deerfield rivers.

☞ **Myles Standish State Forest, Mass.:** Hiking, biking, and horseback trails present opportunities at this state forest at South Carver. Swim and fish after you traverse a trail or two.

☞ **The Taconic Crest Trail, Mass.:** Hike and bike along this trail in the Berkshires that follows the New York/Massachusetts border at Williams College's Hopkins Memorial Forest.

☞ **Franconia Notch State Park, N.H.:** The paved biking trail runs parallel to the hiking route of the Appalachian Trail system in the White Mountains region; the scenery is breathtaking. For a change of pace, try some of the park's hiking trails, which lead to covered bridges, lakes, and clear mountain streams. *FYI:* Franconia and Lincoln; off I-93; 603-823-9930 for trail information.

☞ **Bellevue Avenue and Ocean Drive, R.I.:** For 15 miles, this trail in Newport passes by some of the most extravagant mansions in the nation. If you continue on, you will enjoy lovely ocean views.

☞ **East Bay Bicycle Path, R.I.:** This 10-foot-wide, 14.5-mile-long trail links Providence, Rhode Island, to Bristol, Connecticut. Several state parks are scattered along the way; the trail also follows Veteran's Memorial Parkway in East Providence. Bikers and hikers only.

To Ski or Not to Ski

For winter sports enthusiasts, life without snow may qualify as almost no life at all. Fortunately, ski bums can get more than their fill of the white stuff in New England. The slopes listed below represent a small sampling to get you started on your downhill slide; when you hit bottom is up to you.

Cross-country skiing in Vermont

☞ **Saddleback Mountain, Maine:** The state's second-largest snow resort is located about one hour's drive from Sugarloaf. The 4,116-foot summit boasts a vertical drop of 1,826 feet. The forty or so runs offer challenges for all levels.

☞ **Sugarloaf Mountain U.S.A., Maine:** This is numero uno for skiers in Maine and, perhaps, New England. The skiing is first rate, and the scenery is beautiful.

☞ **Attitash, N.H.:** In Bartlett, this is not only tops for popular skiing, but is also a U.S. Ski Team training center.

☞ **White Mountains, N.H.:** This is some of the best skiing in New Hampshire. Whether you prefer nordic or alpine, at least ten resorts feature downhill runs and cross-country trails.

☞ **Mount Mansfield, Vt.:** At Stowe, this ski area—on Vermont's highest mountain—ranks among the state's best. The Civilian Conservation Corps cut a trail on Mt. Mansfield in 1933. Since then it has been uphill all the way for the ski capital of the East.

☞ **Smugglers' Notch Ski Area, Vt.:** This recreation area includes three main skiable mountains: Morse, Sterling, and Madonna. Mt. Madonna rises 3,668 feet above sea level and boasts a 2,610-foot vertical rise to tempt expert skiers. There are great moguls for the hearty, and even young children won't be left out in the cold. The children's center offers day care, ski lessons, and camp sessions. Smugglers' Notch gained its name courtesy of the smugglers who carried contraband through the "notch" during the War of 1812. *FYI:* 8 miles north of Stowe in Jeffersonville.

Vt. Travel Division

Downhill on Okemo Mountain, Vt.

Race it!

In 1620, Pilgrims in pursuit of religious freedom undertook a dangerous journey by ship from England to the New World. That journey was retraced for sport in 1866 when the Vesta and the Henrietta raced from New England to England. Thus was born the tradition of transatlantic yacht racing. In 1870, the first race of the America's Cup was held in Newport, and today, yacht racing is still a passionate pursuit of New Englanders. Smooth sailing can often be found in Cape Cod Bay or Long Island Sound. The 2,500-mile stretch of Maine's rugged coastline is best seen from on board a graceful windjammer; commercial tours can be arranged in Camden, Maine. *FYI:* 207-236-4404.

R.I. Tourism Division

Sailing off Rhode Island's coast

Go Fish, Go Hunt

Licensing procedures and laws vary from state to state in New England. Contact state agencies to be sure you are informed about current regulations.

Ice fishing on Damariscotta Lake, Maine

Maine Office of Tourism

Connecticut: Department of Environmental Protection, Information, and Education, State Office Building, Hartford, CT 06106.
Maine: Department of Inland Fisheries and Wildlife, 284 State Street, Augusta, ME 04333; Superintendent, Acadia National Park, P.O. Box 177, Bar Harbor, ME, 04609.
Massachusetts: Division of Marine Fisheries, 100 Cambridge Street, Boston, MA 02202.
New Hampshire: Fish and Game Department, 2 Hazen Drive, Concord, NH 03301.
Rhode Island: Division of Fish and Wildlife, Government Center, Tower Hill Road, Wakefield, RI 02879.
Vermont: Department of Fish and Wildlife, 103 South Main Street, 10 South Building, Waterbury, VT 05676.

Go Sporting

Recreational and spectator sports are a perfectly respectable business in the land of the Yankees. Professional baseball, basketball, football, hockey, and tennis teams are well represented, and the daily newspaper sports section is the place to look for short-term, up-to-the-minute scheduling. Boston has more than its fair share: the **Boston Celtics** for basket-

Die-hard golfers can get their strokes in at one of New England's numerous and scenic courses.

Vt. Travel Division

ball (they play in Boston Garden from September through May), the **Boston Bruins** for hockey (you can cheer them on at Boston Garden from October through March), the **Boston Red Sox** for baseball (at Fenway Park, of course, from April to October). The **New England Patriots** hail from Foxboro, Massachusetts, where they play football at Sullivan Stadium.

Rockingham Park, Salem, offers **thoroughbred horse racing** during much of the year.

Vt. Travel Division

Recreation takes many forms, among them a balloon landing in Calais, Vt.

Phineas Taylor Barnum (1810–1891)

P. T. Barnum, the famous American showman, was born in Bethel, Connecticut. In his youth, Barnum held various jobs, but he found his true calling at the age of 25 when he debuted his first sensation, Joice Heth, an 80-year-old former slave who claimed to be twice that old. Barnum opened the American Museum in New York City and was known for his outrageous exhibits and ad campaigns. Gen. Tom Thumb was another major Barnum discovery. Barnum successfully managed Swedish singer Jenny Lind's American debut tour before he retired from show biz in 1855. He served as mayor of Bridgeport, Connecticut, and as a state legislator and survived bankruptcy before he went on to organize "The Greatest Show on Earth."

THE SPIRIT OF NEW ENGLAND

Sea to Sea

Joseph Devenney/Maine Office of Tourism

Harbor, Camden, Maine

The first European settlers traveled by sea to reach the land that would become known as New England. Long before that, Native Americans depended on the coastal fish-filled waters for their survival. Both Native Americans and colonists used weirs—dams, barriers, and simple mesh structures made of branches—to pool water and snare or trap fish. In the mid-1600s, Yankee ships fished the waters off Newfoundland for haddock, cod, and pollack. For New England, fishing and other sea-related commerce formed the heart of trade with Europe. Yankee whaling was centered in Connecticut and southern Massachusetts, China trade merchants were based in New Hampshire and northern Massachusetts, and Maine was the shipbuilding axis for the nation. When you visit the Massachusetts **State House**, take a look at the **Sacred Cod** that hangs in the House Chamber. *FYI:* Mystic Seaport, Mystic, Conn.

Ships and Shipbuilding

Since the beginning of the seventeenth century, the wooden ship has been the foundation of New England's shipbuilding tradition. The first colonists were quick to establish shipyards along the coast where they could assemble small sloops and ketches. By the eighteenth century, they were constructing three-masted schooners that were seaworthy. These sailing vessels were rigged fore and aft, and they were faster and required a smaller crew than square-rigged ships, attributes that came in handy during the American Revolution.

English oppression of colonial New England led to smuggling by colonists, and the swift, navigable schooners were perfectly equipped to evade British ships. During the Revolutionary War, armed schooners, known as Privateers, were authorized by the Continental Congress to pursue enemy ships.

Schooners remained the favorite sailing craft of Canada and the United States from the mid-1800s to the early 1900s. They were crucial to the North Atlantic fishing industry and North American trade until World War I, when power-driven craft outmaneuvered them. *FYI:* There are shipbuilding exhibits at the Penobscot Museum, Maine; Sears Port, 207-548-2529.

Ice Industry

Before the invention of refrigeration in the late nineteenth century, demand was great for block ice harvested in New England north of Boston and in Maine. The ice was transported via ships to the American South, the West Indies, and even as far as India. Winter was harvest time; lakes and ponds were scraped and marked, and blocks (sometimes weighing in at 200 pounds) were cut. Packed in sawdust, the ice was stored until the first thaw enabled ships to load up and sail to warmer destinations. Special airtight hulls in the vessels helped to slow melting.

Glossary of the Sailing Vessel

Schooner: A vessel with two or more masts; sails are rigged fore and aft

Sloop: A vessel with one mast; rigged fore and aft

Ship: A vessel with three or more masts; sails are square-rigged

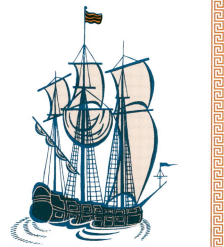

Clipper Ships

Long, narrow, graceful clipper ships with their cloud of sails were built for speed; "clipper" comes from the term "at a fast clip." These wooden sailing vessels appeared between 1820 and 1860

Joseph Devenney/Maine Office of Tourism

Schooner race, Rockland Breakwater

and brought the age of sailing to its zenith. The true Yankee clipper is thought to have emerged with the design and construction of the Ann McKim. Famed New England shipbuilder Donald McKay perfected the Yankee clipper when he built such vessels as the Glory of the Seas and the Flying Cloud.

Donald McKay (1810–1880)

Donald McKay was born in Nova Scotia. At the age of 31, he established his first shipyard in Newburyport, Massachusetts. In 1845, McKay moved to Boston and gained celebrity as designer and builder of some of the world's most beautiful ships. The New World, the Lightning, and the James Baines were McKay clipper ships that set speed records for the England-to-Australia route. In 1869, his ship, Glory of the Seas, made the New York–San Francisco run in 94 days, a new record. McKay constructed several ships for the Union Navy during the War Between the States.

Joseph Devenney/Maine Office of Tourism

Windjammer

The Down-Easter

In the late nineteenth century and early twentieth century, Maine shipyards produced commercial sailing vessels such as the *Down-Easter*, a three-masted square-rigger. These vessels could almost equal the speeds of clipper ships. Great schooners carried bulk cargo such as grain, lumber, and coal from the East Coast to the West Coast via the Cape Horn route.

Summer boat show, Newport, R.I.

R.I. Tourism Division

China Trade

After the American Revolution, free trade with Africa, Europe, and the West Indies became possible for New World entrepreneurs. New England's sailors manned ships that sailed to the Orient as part of the China trade. Silks, tea, porcelains, furs, and sandalwood were only a few of the items of trade collected along the way by adventurous sailors turned explorers.

In 1799, Salem sea merchants organized the **Salem East India Maritime Society**, a group that set up a museum of artifacts collected from around the world in the ship trade. George Peabody gave the society financial aid, and the museum now retains his name. *FYI:* **Peabody Museum**, East India Square, Salem, Mass.

A variety of shops and restaurants are located on **Pickering Wharf**, in Salem. The **Salem Maritime National Historic Site** (directly beyond Pickering Wharf) is a historic waterfront area administered by the National Park Service. The 2,000-foot Derby Wharf—one of forty wharfs that existed a century ago—is still maintained.

Old Ironsides
Don't miss the **USS Constitution**, a.k.a. "Old Ironsides," the oldest commissioned warship in the world, launched in 1797 and restored and berthed at the Charlestown Navy Yard, Boston. Old Ironsides sailed against the British in the War of 1812, and she also encountered Barbary pirates. She retired undefeated. The yard was opened in 1800 to supply ships for the first U.S. Navy.

Whaling

In the 1800s, whale oil extracted from blubber supplied light, soap, and lubricants; other products derived from whales included sperm oil, ambergris, spermaceti, whalebone or baleen (used to make buggy whips, corset stays, and tools), bone meal, meat, and liver oil. Native Americans had hunted whales long before Europeans arrived in New England. In fact, settlers learned some whaling methods from the Indians.

By the mid-seventeenth century, land-based whaling was centered on the coast of New England. Watchtowers were built to sight whales from shore, and the butchering and processing was done on beaches. After an eighteenth-century seaman caught a sperm whale at sea, larger vessels were equipped for long open-ocean whaling voyages. By 1730, the processing of whale carcasses was moved off land to the sea.

Between 1820 and 1860, New England whaling reached its peak. Whaling ports were bustling twenty-four hours a day as ships arrived and departed. New Bedford—the world's greatest whaling port—boasted more than 300 vessels, and Nantucket had more than 80. Provincetown, Mystic, Fairhaven, Stonington, and Edgartown also had whaling fleets.

With over-hunting, the number of whales seriously declined, and voyages took months, sometimes several years. A ship captain was likely to take his wife and children along on the sea journey. *FYI:* New Bedford Whaling Museum, 18 Johnny Cake Hill, New Bedford; 508-997-0046.

Conn. Dept. of Economic Development

The whaler Charles W. Morgan, Mystic, Conn.

Life on a Whaler

Life on board a whaling vessel was rough, overcrowded, and dangerous. Two- and three-masted ships were crewed by 15 or 20 men and carried five or six whale boats on board. When the watch sailor hollered, "Thar she blows!" the boats were lowered and the chase began. A half-dozen men manned each boat, rowing to keep up with the great mammal that was their prey. If the first harpoon struck its target, the boat was towed behind the wounded whale. After the animal died from repeated lance wounds, it was cut-in ship-side, a bloody process that took days. *FYI:* Nantucket Whaling Museum, Broad St.; 508-228-1894.

Sperm Whale *(Physeter catodon)*

The single species of sperm whale—the world's largest toothed mammal—is found in all oceans. The sexually mature male may reach a head and body length of 20 meters (almost 22 yards) and a weight of 50,000 kilograms (about 110,230 pounds), while the female usually measures less than 12 meters (13 yards) and weighs one-third as much as the male.

Sperm whales are usually found in waters where they can feed on squid. Before a dive, these mammals spout and lift their tail flukes high. Yelps, groans, chirps, whistles, clicks, and pings are not unusual forms of communication for sperm whales.

Undoubtedly, humans create the biggest problem for whales. Since the early days of whaling, hundreds of thousands of whales have been killed. Their blubber has been used for gelatin, margarine, lamp oil, and glue. These days, other products like petroleum take the place of whale blubber. Commercial hunting of sperm whales was halted by 1985. And now, because so many people want to see whales up close, scientists are studying how tourism may affect these mighty giants. *FYI:* Whale Watches; Captain John Boats, Plymouth; 508-746-2643, April through November.

Witch Trials and Errors

Although the Salem witch hunts occurred roughly three centuries ago, in 1692, sociologists and historians do not agree on the cause, meaning, or relevance of this peculiar period of American history—but then, neither did those men who witnessed the trials and wrote about them. That year of fanatical accusation and judgment is still shrouded in mystery and superstition.

The scare seems to have started in the home of Reverend Samuel Parris. Tituba, the African American domestic servant who worked in the minister's house, kept young village children entertained with supernatural folk tales. After months of stories, some of the children began to behave strangely, exhibiting hysterical symptoms such as convulsions. When the malady spread, the town physician, Dr.

Griggs, used up his repertoire of remedies and pronounced the children bewitched by Satan; the Salem clergy agreed.

The children were then encouraged to identify their tormentors, and the first three "witches" were named: Tituba, Sara Good (the local "hag"), and Sarah Osbourne, a woman of status who had besmirched her reputation by living with a man before she married him.

Tituba confessed and announced to the court that many others in the village had conspired with Satan. At this point, accusations snowballed, and soon the jail was crowded with suspected witches—both male and female. When the hysteria spread to nearby Andover and other towns, colonial officials stepped in. They established a Court of Oyer and Terminer to try the accused witches. Those who confessed remained in prison; those who refused were hanged.

When Samuel Wilard, president of Harvard College, pastor of

the First Church of Boston, and a highly prominent male member of the community, was accused of being a witch—a turning point—the entire proceedings were brought into question. *FYI:* **Salem Witch Museum** has exhibits that trace the events of the witch hunts of 1692 and 1693; 19½ Washington Square North, Salem, Mass. **Witch House**, the Salem home of Judge Corwin, a witch trial judge, where more than 200 accused witches were brought to chambers for a preliminary hearing; 310½ Essex Street.

Cotton Mather (1663–1728)

Puritan clergyman and writer Cotton Mather was born in Boston and graduated from Harvard College. He was ordained in 1685 and served as pastor at North Church, Boston, after his father, Increase Mather, died. His numerous writings made him one of New England's most celebrated and influential Puritans. Today, Mather is generally remembered for his work, *Memorable Providences relating to Witchcraft and Possessions* (1689), which stirred the hysteria that led to the Salem witch trials of 1692. He penned a second work about Satanic possession in 1693, *Wonders of the Invisible World*. Although Mather is seen as the archetypal intolerant Puritan, he was deeply interested in science and was influential in the founding of Yale University.

Robert Calef (1648–1719)

Robert Calef was probably born in England and journeyed to New England, where he became a Boston cloth merchant. He is known for his work, *More Wonders of the Invisible World* (1700), which was a scathing response to Cotton Mather's work of 1689, a condemnation of the prevailing view of witchcraft, and an indictment of Mather's role in the witch trials. When Boston printers refused to publish Calef's book, it was printed in London.

Graveyards and Gravestones

Gravestones provided an expressive outlet for Puritan stonecutters who led otherwise strict, austere lives. Row upon row of headstones decorate New England's old and historic burial grounds; their designs indicate stylistic preferences throughout the centuries.

Early traditional designs included winged skulls, cherubim, hearts, the hourglass, the sun, and other symbols of death and resurrection. Realistic scenes of death and detailed portraits of the deceased became popular motifs during the eighteenth century. Weeping willows, Grecian urns, and other romantic symbols of mortality were used frequently during the nineteenth century.

Cemeteries are everywhere in New England. Far from being grim reminders of death and dying, they are pastoral greens where flowers and trees are usually in abundance. Boston, Lexington, Boxborough, Newport, Newburyport, and New London are only a few of the towns with burial grounds whose headstones represent fine examples of the art of stone carving. A few cemeteries and graves of note are listed below.

Old Burying Ground, Maine: Bordered by a typical New England stone wall, the Old Burying Ground (a.k.a. Old York Cemetery) in York contains many seventeenth-century tombstones. The Witch's Tomb (see next page) is of special note.

Boston Common, Mass.: This all-purpose and well-used green was formerly used as a militia training ground, a pasture, and a graveyard. The markers still show you the way to the cemetery.

Copp's Hill Burying Ground, Mass.: This graveyard is dotted with the headstones of early Bostonians. Cotton Mather is buried here. Look for headstones marked by British bullets. *FYI:* Behind Old North, between Charter and Hull streets, Boston.

Graves

Witches Tomb, Maine: This grave—marked by a horizontal slab and two vertical slabs—is within the boundaries of the Old Burying Ground in York. This curious positioning of stones was thought to keep the witch from escaping its final place of rest.

Rebecca Nurse Homestead, Mass.: This is the Salem abode of an accused witch who was hanged even though townspeople had gathered a petition protesting her innocence. She is buried in an unmarked grave in the field outside her homestead. *FYI:* 149 Pine Street, Danvers, 4 miles outside Salem.

Conn. Dept. of Economic Development

Old New-Gate Prison was Connecticut's first state prison; it held Tories during the American Revolution.

Dungeons and Gaols

Puritans practiced an effective form of punishment; they placed the transgressor in stocks (heavy wooden frames that had holes to confine hands and feet) or the pillory (a device that had holes in which the head and hands were locked), or they applied the lash. When these public punishments became ineffectual in dealing with the larger community and the increase in criminal problems, jails, or gaols, were put into use.

Lincoln County Museum and Old Jail, Maine: This forbidding stone edifice was constructed in 1809 and housed roughly forty prisoners in its cells. The third floor was the last stop for debtors, women prisoners, and those who were judged insane. *FYI:* Federal Street, Wiscasset.

Old Gaol Museum, Maine: This stone dungeon dates to 1720. Its purpose was to incarcerate anyone who offended the province of Maine. It soon needed expansion; cells were added, along with quarters for the jailer and family. Note the slivers cut into the thick walls where sunlight might occasionally enter. *FYI:* Colonial York.

Museums

Unusual museums seem to be a specialty in New England. Whether you want to learn about clocks, railroads, cars, or the circus, there's a museum for you.

Conn. Dept. of Economic Development

Shore Line Trolley Museum, East Haven, Conn.

☛ **American Clock and Watch Museum, Conn.:** American clocks in general, and Connecticut clocks in particular, are on display here. Bristol, Connecticut, produced more than 200,000 clocks in 1860, and home state clockmakers such as Eli Terry and Seth Thomas revolutionized the timepiece industry by creating standardized wooden parts. Suddenly clocks were affordable. *FYI:* 100 Maple Street, Bristol.

☛ **Barnum Museum, Conn.:** It is no surprise that the famous P. T. Barnum would have collected circus memorabilia, much of which is on display here. Included are exhibits of furnishings belonging to Tom Thumb (a local son). Another highlight is the **Brinley Miniature Circus**, which consists of more than 500,000 carved circus figurines. *FYI:* 820 Main Street, Bridgeport.

☛ **Wells Auto Museum, Maine:** More than sixty antique cars, bicycles, and motorcycles are on exhibit. *FYI:* Route 1, Wells; 207-646-9064.

☛ **Shelburne Museum, Vt.:** Thirty-five historic structures house collections of paintings, textiles, folk arts, toys, and furniture, among other things. A railroad train and a side-wheel steamer are also on site. *FYI:* Route 7, Shelburne; 802-985-3344.

Libraries

☛ **Beinecke Rare Book and Manuscript Library, Conn.:** Uncommon books and manuscripts, including an edition of the Gutenberg Bible, are housed within these walls. *FYI:* Wall Street, Yale University, New Haven; 203-432-2977.

☛ **Boston Public Library, Mass.:** The General Library is part of the new wing designed in 1972 by Philip Johnson. The earlier Renaissance Revival structure designed in 1895 by McKim, Mead and White houses the Research Library. In addition to extensive reading material, look for paintings by John Singer Sargent, Edwin Abbey, and Puvis de Chavannes, as well as statues by Bela Pratt. *FYI:* At Boylston and Exeter streets.

☛ **Hayden Memorial Library, Mass.:** This library houses an extensive research collection. *FYI:* Massachusetts Institute of Technology (MIT), Cambridge.

☛ **Houghton Library and Pusey Library, Mass.:** These hold the university's rare books and manuscripts and its archives, respectively. *FYI:* Harvard Yard, Harvard University, Cambridge.

☛ **Schlesinger Library, Mass.:** This library contains the nation's most expansive collection of women's studies titles; it is adjacent to the Bunting Institute, the fellowship program for women artists, scholars, and writers. *FYI:* Radcliffe College, Cambridge.

☛ **Widener Memorial Library, Mass.:** This is the world's largest university library, and it honors the former Harvard student who was on board the ill-fated Titanic when she sank. *FYI:* Harvard Yard, Harvard University, Cambridge.

☛ **St. Johnsbury Athenaeum, Vt.:** This is a notable library and art gallery. *FYI:* 30 Main Street, Saint Johnsbury; 802-748-8291.

☛ **Starr Library, Vt.:** This university library possesses a collection of works by poet Robert Frost. *FYI:* Middlebury College.

Higher Learning Trivia Quiz

1) Poet Emily Dickinson attended _____ before she settled permanently in Amherst.
  a) Amherst College **b)** Mount Holyoke College **c)** Vassar College
2) The innovative Hampshire College in the Pioneer Valley, Massachusetts, was founded in _____.
  a) 1662 **b)** 1879 **c)** 1971
3) The Massachusetts Institute of Technology, or MIT, was founded in 1861 by natural scientist _____.
  a) Ann Radcliffe **b)** William Barton Rogers **c)** George Peabody

ANSWERS: 1) b 2) c 3) b

KIDS' ADVENTURES

Kidding Around

Fort Edgecomb, Maine:

You are welcome to picnic on the grounds of this fort, which was constructed during the War of 1812 to protect the town of Wiscasset. There is an octagonal blockhouse that overlooks the Sheepscot River and Westport Island. *FYI:* 1 mile southeast of Wiscasset; open Memorial Day through Labor Day.

Kids and adults alike will enjoy the Whatever Race held annually on the Kennebec River, Gardiner, Maine

Paul Revere House, Mass.: If you've read your history, you'll want to visit the Boston home of American hero Paul Revere. This was the starting point of his historic ride to Lexington on April 18, 1775. This clapboard home is the oldest standing building in Boston. It was nearly 100 years old when Paul Revere purchased it in 1770. *FYI:* Boston; 617-523-2338.

Hart Nautical Collections, Mass.: Located on the MIT campus in Cambridge, this collection is part of the MIT Museum. Ship models and engine models chronicle the evolution of the shipbuilding industry. This is for serious students of things nautical. *FYI:* 77 Massachusetts Avenue.

Mass. Office of Travel and Tourism

Kids can get a glimpse of history at Plimouth Plantation, Plymouth, Mass.

Morgan Horse Farm, Vt.: In the 1780s, schoolmaster Justin Morgan made equine history when he took a horse in trade for a debt. Morgan's colt sired a new breed of American horse, the Morgan. The descendants of this stallion are known for their speed, strength, agility, even temperament, courage, and heart. The Morgan horse became Vermont's official state animal in 1961. Since 1951 the Morgan Horse Farm has been operated by the University of Vermont. Horse lovers are welcome to tour the nineteenth-century barn where Morgans are still housed and trained. *FYI:* In Weybridge, 1½ miles north of Middlebury; open May through October.

Each summer, Native Americans and modern colonists gather to re-create and celebrate seventeenth- and eighteenth-century life along the Connecticut River in Durham, Conn.

State and local country fairs are great places to relax and enjoy new places and faces, as at the Common Ground Fair in Maine

Ferries, Railways, and other Modes of Go!

Because kids love to be on the go, New England's numerous ferries, trolleys, and trams are a great way for family members of all ages to see the sights.

Conn. Dept. of Economic Development

Enjoy a ride aboard the Valley Railroad Steam Locomotive that travels the countryside between Essex and Chester, Conn.

Ferries

☛ **Bridgeport, Conn.–Port Jefferson Ferry:** Bridgeport, Conn. to Port Jefferson, Long Island. *FYI:* Union Square Dock, Bridgeport; 203-367-3043.

☛ **Rockland, Maine–North Haven Ferry:** Cruise Pulpit Harbor. *FYI:* Route 1, Rockland; 207-594-5543.

☛ **Rockland, Maine–Vinalhaven Ferry:** excursion to Vinalhaven and tour of island. *FYI:* Route 1, Rockland; 207-594-5543.

☛ **Woods Hole, Mass.–Martha's Vineyard Ferry:** Excursion to towns of Vineyard Haven and Oak Bluffs on the island. *FYI:* Woods Hole; 508-477-8600.

☛ **Woods Hole, Mass.–Nantucket Ferry:** 3-hour excursion to a resort island. *FYI:* Woods Hole; 508-477-8600.

☛ **Burlington, Vt.–Port Kent Ferry:** Cross to Port Kent, N.Y. *FYI:* Off I-89, Burlington; 802-864-9804.

☛ **Charlotte, Vt.–Essex Ferry:** To Essex, N.Y. *FYI:* Route F-5, Charlotte; 802-864-9804.

☛ **Grande Isle, Vt.–Plattsburgh Ferry:** To Plattsburgh, N.Y. *FYI:* Off I-89, Grand Isle; 802-864-9804.

☛ **Shoreham, Vt.–Ticonderoga Ferry:** Cross Lake Champlain. *FYI:* Shorewell Ferries dock, Shoreham; 802-897-7999.

The SS *Ticonderoga* and the Colchester Reef Lighthouse can be seen at the Shelburne Museum, Shelburne, Vt. The side-wheeler steam ship cruised Lake Champlain for almost 50 years. It carried people and freight. You can still board her today. Another treat awaits railroad buffs: the Shelburne Railroad Station is a classic example of Victorian style. Additional sights include a traditional wooden round barn and a Circus Parade Building which houses carousel horses, circus posters, and a hand-carved miniature circus.

Vt. Travel Division

Trams, Trolleys, and Railways

Connecticut Electric Railway Association Warehouse Point Trolley Museum: Railway cars dating from the early 1900s to 1947 are on view. There's also a trolley ride and a gift shop. *FYI:* 58 North Road, East Windsor; 203-627-6540.

Shore Line Trolley Museum, Conn.: Take a trolley ride and stop to picnic. *FYI:* 17 River Street, East Haven; 203-467-6927.

Valley Railroad Company, Conn.: Excursions aboard a vintage steam train from Essex to Chester. There's also a riverboat cruise. *FYI:* Route 9, Essex; 203-767-0103.

Seashore Trolley Museum, Maine: Trolley for twenty minutes and then learn all about the restoration of these electric vehicles. *FYI:* Log Cabin Road, Kennebunkport; 207-967-2712.

Mount Mansfield Gondola, Vt.: Ride to the summit of the great mountain in an enclosed gondola. *FYI:* Off Route 180, Stowe; 802-253-7311.

Stowe Alpine Slide, Vt.: Chair-lift to the top of the peak and head down by sled! *FYI:* Off Route 108, Stowe; 802-253-7311.

Vt. Travel Division

SKIwee-affiliated programs at Stratton Mountain, Vt., teach kids the basics

INDEX

Other Books from John Muir Publications

Travel Books by Rick Steves

Asia Through the Back Door, 4th ed., 400 pp. $16.95

Europe 101: History and Art for the Traveler, 4th ed., 372 pp. $15.95

Europe Through the Back Door, 12th ed., 434 pp. $17.95

Europe Through the Back Door Phrase Book: French, 112 pp. $4.95

Europe Through the Back Door Phrase Book: German, 112 pp. $4.95

Europe Through the Back Door Phrase Book: Italian, 112 pp. $4.95

Europe Through the Back Door Phrase Book: Spanish & Portuguese, 288 pp. $4.95

Mona Winks: Self-Guided Tours of Europe's Top Museums, 2nd ed., 456 pp. $16.95

See the 2 to 22 Days series to follow for other Rick Steves titles.

A Natural Destination Series

Belize: A Natural Destination, 2nd ed., 304 pp. $16.95

Costa Rica: A Natural Destination, 3rd ed., 320 pp. $16.95 (available 8/94)

Guatemala: A Natural Destination, 336 pp. $16.95

Undiscovered Islands Series

Undiscovered Islands of the Caribbean, 3rd ed., 264 pp. $14.95

Undiscovered Islands of the Mediterranean, 2nd ed., 256 pp. $13.95

Undiscovered Islands of the U.S. and Canadian West Coast, 288 pp. $12.95

For Birding Enthusiasts

The Birder's Guide to Bed and Breakfasts, U.S. and Canada, 288 pp. $15.95

The Visitor's Guide to the Birds of the Central National Parks: U.S. and Canada, 400 pp. $15.95 (available 8/94)

The Visitor's Guide to the Birds of the Eastern National Parks: U.S. and Canada, 400 pp. $15.95

The Visitor's Guide to the Birds of the Rocky Mountain National Parks, U.S. and Canada, 432 pp. $15.95

Unique Travel Series
Each is 112 pages and $10.95 paper.

Unique Arizona (available 9/94)
Unique California (available 9/94)
Unique Colorado
Unique Florida
Unique New England
Unique New Mexico
Unique Texas

2 to 22 Days Series
Each title offers 22 flexible daily itineraries useful for planning vacations of any length. Included are "must see" attractions as well as hidden "jewels."

2 to 22 Days in the American Southwest, 1994 ed., 192 pp. $10.95

2 to 22 Days in Asia, 1994 ed., 176 pp. $10.95

2 to 22 Days in Australia, 1994 ed., 192 pp. $10.95

2 to 22 Days in California, 1994 ed., 192 pp. $10.95

2 to 22 Days in Eastern Canada, 1994 ed., 192 pp. $12.95

2 to 22 Days in Europe, 1994 ed., 304 pp. $14.95

2 to 22 Days in Florida, 1994 ed., 192 pp. $10.95

2 to 22 Days in France, 1994 ed., 192 pp. $10.95

2 to 22 Days in Germany, Austria, and Switzerland, 1994 ed., 240 pp. $12.95

2 to 22 Days in Great Britain, 1994 ed., 208 pp. $10.95

2 to 22 Days Around the Great Lakes, 1994 ed., 192 pp. $10.95

2 to 22 Days in Hawaii, 1994 ed., 192 pp. $10.95

2 to 22 Days in Italy, 1994 ed., 208 pp. $10.95

2 to 22 Days in New England, 1994 ed., 192 pp. $10.95

2 to 22 Days in New Zealand, 1994 ed., 192 pp. $10.95

2 to 22 Days in Norway, Sweden, and Denmark, 1994 ed., 192 pp. $10.95

2 to 22 Days in the Pacific Northwest, 1994 ed., 192 pp. $10.95

2 to 22 Days in the Rockies, 1994 ed., 192 pp. $10.95

2 to 22 Days in Spain and Portugal, 1994 ed., 208 pp. $10.95

2 to 22 Days in Texas, 1994 ed., 192 pp. $10.95

2 to 22 Days in Thailand, 1994 ed., 192 pp. $10.95

22 Days (or More) Around the World, 1994 ed., 264 pp. $13.95

Other Terrific Travel Titles

The 100 Best Small Art Towns in America, 256 pp. $12.95 (available 8/94)

Elderhostels: The Students' Choice, 2nd ed., 304 pp. $15.95

Environmental Vacations: Volunteer Projects to Save the Planet, 2nd ed., 248 pp. $16.95

A Foreign Visitor's Guide to America, 224 pp. $12.95

Great Cities of Eastern Europe, 256 pp. $16.95

Indian America: A Traveler's Companion, 3rd ed., 432 pp. $18.95

Interior Furnishings Southwest, 256 pp. $19.95

Opera! The Guide to Western Europe's Great Houses, 296 pp. $18.95

Paintbrushes and Pistols: How the Taos Artists Sold the West, 288 pp. $17.95

The People's Guide to Mexico, 9th ed., 608 pp. $18.95

Ranch Vacations: The Complete Guide to Guest and Resort, Fly-Fishing, and Cross-Country Skiing Ranches, 3rd ed., 528 pp. $19.95

The Shopper's Guide to Art and Crafts in the Hawaiian Islands, 272 pp. $13.95

The Shopper's Guide to Mexico, 224 pp. $9.95

Understanding Europeans, 272 pp. $14.95

A Viewer's Guide to Art: A Glossary of Gods, People, and Creatures, 144 pp. $10.95

Watch It Made in the U.S.A.: A Visitor's Guide to the Companies that Make Your Favorite Products, 272 pp. $16.95 (available 7/94)

Parenting Titles

Being a Father: Family, Work, and Self, 176 pp. $12.95
Preconception: A Woman's Guide to Preparing for Pregnancy and Parenthood, 232 pp. $14.95

Schooling at Home: Parents, Kids, and Learning, 264 pp., $14.95

Teens: A Fresh Look, 240 pp. $14.95

Automotive Titles

The Greaseless Guide to Car Care Confidence, 224 pp. $14.95

How to Keep Your Datsun/Nissan Alive, 544 pp. $21.95

How to Keep Your Subaru Alive, 480 pp. $21.95

How to Keep Your Toyota Pickup Alive, 392 pp. $21.95

How to Keep Your VW Alive, 15th ed., 464 pp. $21.95

TITLES FOR YOUNG READERS AGES 8 AND UP

American Origins Series
Each is 48 pages and $12.95 hardcover.
Tracing Our Chinese Roots
Tracing Our German Roots
Tracing Our Irish Roots
Tracing Our Italian Roots
Tracing Our Japanese Roots
Tracing Our Jewish Roots
Tracing Our Polish Roots

Bizarre & Beautiful Series
Each is 48 pages and $14.95 hardcover.
Bizarre & Beautiful Ears
Bizarre & Beautiful Eyes
Bizarre & Beautiful Feelers
Bizarre & Beautiful Noses
Bizarre & Beautiful Tongues

Environmental Titles

Habitats: Where the Wild Things Live, 48 pp. $9.95
The Indian Way: Learning to Communicate with Mother Earth, 114 pp. $9.95

Rads, Ergs, and Cheeseburgers: The Kids' Guide to Energy and the Environment, 108 pp. $13.95

The Kids' Environment Book: What's Awry and Why, 192 pp. $13.95

Extremely Weird Series
Each is 48 pages and $9.95 paper. $12.95 hardcover editions available 8/94.
Extremely Weird Bats
Extremely Weird Birds
Extremely Weird Endangered Species
Extremely Weird Fishes
Extremely Weird Frogs
Extremely Weird Insects
Extremely Weird Mammals
Extremely Weird Micro Monsters
Extremely Weird Primates
Extremely Weird Reptiles
Extremely Weird Sea Creatures
Extremely Weird Snakes
Extremely Weird Spiders

Kidding Around Travel Series
All are 64 pages and $9.95 paper, except for *Kidding Around Spain* and *Kidding Around the National Parks of the Southwest*, which are 108 pages and $12.95 paper.
Kidding Around Atlanta
Kidding Around Boston, 2nd ed.
Kidding Around Chicago, 2nd ed.
Kidding Around the Hawaiian Islands
Kidding Around London
Kidding Around Los Angeles

Kidding Around the National Parks of the Southwest
Kidding Around New York City, 2nd ed.
Kidding Around Paris
Kidding Around Philadelphia
Kidding Around San Diego
Kidding Around San Francisco
Kidding Around Santa Fe
Kidding Around Seattle
Kidding Around Spain
Kidding Around Washington, D.C., 2nd ed.

Kids Explore Series
Written by kids for kids, all are $9.95 paper.
Kids Explore America's African American Heritage, 128 pp.

Kids Explore the Gifts of Children with Special Needs, 128 pp.

Kids Explore America's Hispanic Heritage, 112 pp.

Kids Explore America's Japanese American Heritage, 144 pp.

Masters of Motion Series
Each is 48 pages and $9.95 paper.
How to Drive an Indy Race Car
How to Fly a 747
How to Fly the Space Shuttle

Rainbow Warrior Artists Series
Each is 48 pages and $14.95 hardcover.
Native Artists of Africa
Native Artists of Europe (available 8/94)
Native Artists of North America

Rough and Ready Series
Each is 48 pages and $12.95 hardcover.
Rough and Ready Cowboys
Rough and Ready Homesteaders
Rough and Ready Loggers (available 7/94)
Rough and Ready Outlaws and Lawmen (available 6/94)
Rough and Ready Prospectors
Rough and Ready Railroaders

X-ray Vision Series
Each is 48 pages and $9.95 paper.
Looking Inside the Brain
Looking Inside Cartoon Animation
Looking Inside Caves and Caverns
Looking Inside Sports Aerodynamics
Looking Inside Sunken Treasures
Looking Inside Telescopes and the Night Sky

Ordering Information
Please check your local bookstore for our books, or call **1-800-888-7504** to order direct. All orders are shipped via UPS; see chart below to calculate your shipping charge for U.S. destinations. **No post office boxes please; we must have a street address to ensure delivery**. If the book you request is not available, we will hold your check until we can ship it. Foreign orders will be shipped surface rate unless otherwise requested; please enclose $3 for the first item and $1 for each additional item.

For U.S. Orders Totaling	Add
Up to $15.00	$4.25
$15.01 to $45.00	$5.25
$45.01 to $75.00	$6.25
$75.01 or more	$7.25

Methods of Payment
Check, money order, American Express, MasterCard, or Visa. We cannot be responsible for cash sent through the mail. For credit card orders, include your card number, expiration date, and your signature, or call **1-800-888-7504**. American Express card orders can only be shipped to billing address of cardholder. Sorry, no C.O.D.'s. Residents of sunny New Mexico, add 6.125% tax to total.

Address all orders and inquiries to:
John Muir Publications
P.O. Box 613
Santa Fe, NM 87504
(505) 982-4078
(800) 888-7504